sushi

sushi

vicki liley

whitecap

This edition published in Canada by Whitecap Books Ltd.
For more information, contact

Whitecap Books
351 Lynn Avenue
North Vancouver, British Columbia, Canada
V7J 2C4

Created and produced by Lansdowne Publishing
www.lansdownepublishing.com.au
sales@lanspub.com.au

Commissioned by Deborah Nixon
Text, styling and photography: Vicki Liley
Step-by-step photography: Alan Benson
Cover and internal design: Bettina Hodgson
Layout: The Modern Art Production Group
Editor: Judith Dunham
Production: Sally Stokes and Eleanor Cant
Project Coordinator: Kate Merrifield

ISBN 1-55825-741-7
Cataloging-in-Publication data available upon request

Set in Humanist in QuarkXPress
Printed in Singapore by Tien Wah Press (Pte) Ltd)

contents

introduction

Sushi, though it may seem humble, is always prepared with great care and is beautifully presented at the table. Given these qualities, it is easy to appreciate the Japanese tradition that food should satisfy all the senses. In Japan, sushi is considered an everyday food. It has enormous variety in both the ingredients used and the different ways it is assembled.

Traditional sushi chefs train long and hard to master the skills necessary for their profession. They learn how to select, handle, preserve and prepare ingredients, and they practice an array of time-honored techniques for making sushi. The idea of preparing sushi might seem intimidating, but once you learn about the basic ingredients and how they are combined, you will find that sushi is easy to assemble at home and that it makes an impressive and delicious meal to serve your family and friends.

Sushi has nutritional advantages as well. Oily fish such as tuna and salmon are a rich source of omega-3 fatty acids, which are highly beneficial in the prevention of heart disease. Most varieties of fresh fish are excellent sources of vitamin B12, essential for building and maintaining healthy cells. Fresh ginger aids in digestion, as does vinegar, which also has antibacterial qualities. Nori, made of seaweed, contains protein, minerals (especially iodine) and vitamins A, B1, B2, B6 and C. The average life expectancy in Japan is among the highest in the world.

The term sushi refers to dishes based on sumeshi, or cooled vinegared rice. The main ingredient is fresh, seasonal fish. In fact, sushi originated as a way of preserving fish. No one knows exactly when sushi was invented, but fish was being pickled with rice in Southeast Asia as early as the fifth century BCE. According to some historians, sushi came to Japan with the introduction of rice cultivation in the fourth century BCE. Others believe that Buddhist priests training in China in the seventh century CE brought sushi with them on their return to Japan.

Later, layers of carp and rice, called nare-zushi, placed in a jar were used as a form of tax payment. The jar was sealed and the contents left to ferment for up to a year. When the time came to open the jar, the fish was removed and eaten, and the rice discarded. This form of sushi can still be found in Japan. Methods of fermentation have developed considerably since then, but the layering of ingredients—rice, fish and vegetables—eventually evolved into the form of sushi we know today.

Sushi is now eaten worldwide as a snack, starter, main course or party food. It is made in many different forms, from rolled, pressed and hand-formed sushi to bowls of vinegared rice scattered with fish and vegetables, known as chirashi-zushi. The rice is usually prepared first, then shaped or molded before the other ingredients are added. When served, sushi is presented in artful arrangements on a platter or on individual dishes. Thin slices of pickled ginger, a small mound of Japanese horseradish called wasabi and soy sauce are offered as accompaniments.

When eating sushi, you can use either your fingers or chopsticks. Contrary to popular belief, the wasabi should not be mixed with the soy sauce. Doing so dilutes the flavors of the two condiments. Instead, a small amount of wasabi is dabbed onto the sushi, which is then dipped into soy sauce. Using too much of either will overwhelm the fresh ingredients that give sushi its delicate tastes. The pickled ginger is consumed between types of sushi to cleanse the palate.

The growing number of sushi restaurants outside Japan attest to the worldwide popularity of this appetizing food. Whether you already make sushi at home or are attempting it for the first time, you will find many enticing recipes in this book. Some might take a bit of practice to master, but most are easy to prepare on the first try.

equipment

For making sushi at home, you will want to have the following basic equipment, which is available at Japanese specialty stores and Asian supermarkets. You may already have some items, such as a chopping board, on hand in your kitchen.

bamboo rolling mat

Made from thin bamboo sticks woven together with string, the *makisu* is essential for making rolled sushi. The mats are inexpensive and are available in two sizes, small and large. The recipes in this book use a large mat, which measures about 9 $\frac{1}{2}$ inches (24 cm) square.

chopping board

Raw ingredients like fish, shrimp (prawns) and vegetables are prepared on a wooden chopping board. A clean dry board is also required for assembling finished sushi rolls. You will want to have a selection of good-quality boards. They should be washed well after each use and allowed to dry thoroughly.

fan

A handheld fan or electric fan is used to quickly cool sushi rice. A piece of firm cardboard works well as a substitute.

Japanese vegetable slicer

Made of plastic, the slicer comes with interchangeable blades for slicing and shredding vegetables. There is no substitute utensil for the slicer, though the French mandoline is similar.

knives

Japanese chefs generally use three knives: a vegetable knife, a fish knife and a cleaver. The knives are as precious to a sushi chef as a sword is to a samurai warrior. Chefs spare no expense on knives and always make sure the blades are sharp. You may prefer to rely on the knives you already have, but you will want to have them sharpened by a professional. Dull knives tear delicate fish and finished sushi, as will serrated knives.

omelet pan

In Japan, omelets are traditionally made in a square frying pan that generally measures 8 inches (20 cm) square (pictured page 35). Some pans are rectangular. As a substitute, you can use an 8-inch (20-cm) round frying pan, then trim the cooked omelet into a square or rectangle to suit individual recipes.

pressed sushi mold

Traditionally made from cypress, the mold, called *oshibako,* has a top, a base and sides that can be removed when unmolding pressed sushi. Molds are square or rectangular and come in many sizes. Some are plastic. Wooden molds need to be soaked in cold water for 10 minutes and wiped dry before use to prevent rice from sticking to them. To clean a wooden mold, rinse thoroughly with cold water; do not use detergent. Dry completely before storing in a cool, dark place. As a substitute, use a small springform pan or plastic food-storage container of similar dimensions and line it with plastic wrap.

rice paddle

A flat, round paddle, or *shamoji*, traditionally made from bamboo, is used for tossing rice in a wooden rice tub and for serving rice. Soak in cold water for 5 minutes to prevent the rice from sticking to it.

rice tub

Made from cypress boards held together with copper wire, this tub, called *hangiri,* is specially designed for preparing sushi rice. The broad shape and low sides speed the process of cooling the rice and folding in the vinegar mixture. Because the wood is porous, it absorbs excess moisture, which helps give sushi rice its characteristic glossy appearance. Prior to use, the tub should be filled with cold water and allowed to stand for 5 minutes, then wiped dry. Clean the tub with cold water, not detergent, and dry completely before storing in a cool, dark place. A wide, shallow, nonmetallic bowl may be substituted for the wooden tub.

serving ware

Only the simplest serving ware is used for sushi, as the food should be the star of the presentation. The Japanese prefer square shapes, but round plates can give variation to a table setting. Wooden boards in different finishes make an easy and attractive way to bring sushi to the table. Chopsticks, chopstick rests and small sauce dishes are also essential for serving.

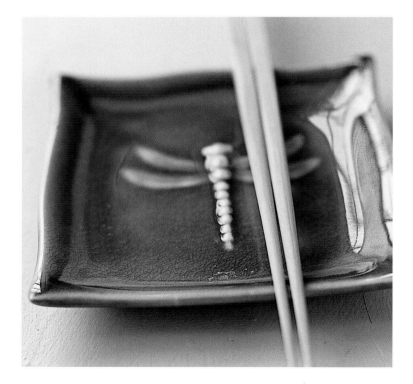

ingredients

fresh fish

When selecting fish for making sushi, freshness is an absolute requirement. Check with the markets in your area to make sure that they carry sashimi-grade seafood or arrange to special-order it.

The Japanese prefer to purchase whole fish, then fillet and slice it just prior to serving, but this is often not practical when making sushi at home. Nevertheless, looking at a whole fish in the market, before the fishmonger prepares it for sale, will give you clues to its freshness. The eyes should be clear and bright, not cloudy. The gills should be bright pink-red and moist, not black-red, and the body should be firm and springy, not spongy and sticky. The fish should smell clean, not unpleasantly fishy. Fillets should be moist, without any signs of discoloration or dryness. Like whole fish, they should have an appealing smell of the sea.

When you go shopping, make fish your last purchase, to ensure that is out of the refrigerator as briefly as possible. You can also put it in an insulated cooler for the trip home.

popular varieties

blue fin tuna

The Japanese classify *maguro* as a red-meat fish. It is usually divided into two sections, the upper and the belly, then is graded and priced according to its fat content. The belly, with the highest amount of fat, is the most prized and the most expensive.

bonito

Bonito is related to tuna, but belongs to the mackerel family. Dried and shaved it is used to make dashi, Japanese stock. For sushi or sashimi, the skin is usually left on. It has a full-rich flavor.

John Dory

Available outside Japan, John Dory (*mato dai*) has firm, delicate white flesh suitable for sushi.

mackerel

Possessing a strong, intense flavor and rich, oily texture, mackerel, or *saba,* is traditionally salted, then marinated in rice vinegar (page 32).

red snapper

Japanese consider the *tai* the best fish in the sea. Its firm, delicately flavored, pink and white flesh is ideal for sushi.

salmon

Widely available, salmon (*sake*) is easily recognized by its silken, firm pink-red flesh. It is appreciated for its rich texture and delicate flavor.

sea bass

A prized fish in Japan, sea bass, or *suzuki,* is also known as *shusse uo,* meaning "advancement in life." The sea bass is associated with success due to its life cycle, which begins in fresh water and culminates in the ocean. The thick, firm white flesh has a subtle flavor and is ideal for hand-formed sushi.

shrimp

Jumbo shrimps (king prawns), known as *ebi,* turn an attractive bright pink and white when cooked and are used in many styles of sushi: rolled, hand formed, hand rolled and scattered. They require special preparation (page 30) to ensure that they do not curl when cooked.

Fresh shrimp are always the best choice, but most shrimp on the market are "fresh frozen," indicating that they were frozen on the boat just after they were caught. When the shrimp are thawed, they are as good as fresh. Even sushi bars in Japan buy frozen shrimp when fresh are unavailable. Thawed shrimp should be used within a day or two and should not be refrozen.

fish roe (pictured)

Fish eggs, such as flying fish roe and lumpfish caviar, are an ingredient in sushi and are used to decorate scattered sushi.

Tobiko, the small, bright orange roe from flying fish, is the most popular choice in Japan for its superior flavor and crunchy texture. It is expensive, and sold fresh or frozen by weight or in tiny containers. Lumpfish caviar, a less costly alternative, is black or bright red and is sold in small jars.

Salmon roe is available in small jars or can be purchased by weight. It is very expensive and should be used in small amounts. Soaking the roe in a little sake for 1 minute helps separate the eggs, making them easier to handle.

Store all fish roe, covered, in the refrigerator and use within four or five days.

eel (pictured)

A very popular food in Japan, eel, or *unagi,* is never eaten raw, even in sushi. The Japanese have an ancient belief that eating eel will keep them healthy from that day throughout the coming year. Thousands of tons of eel are consumed in Japan annually.

Preparing eel requires skill. Traditionally it is filleted and steamed, then skewered and dipped in a sweet sauce of soy sauce, sugar and reduced eel stock. It is then cooked over a charcoal fire. The results have a rich, sweet, nutty flavor and a tender texture. Most of the eel you see in sushi bars outside Japan is imported, already prepared, from Japan.

Eel is available vacuum packed or frozen at Japanese markets. To prepare the eel, remove it from the package and thread it onto bamboo skewers so it keeps its shape. Cook under a preheated broiler (grill) for 2–3 minutes or microwave until heated through. Remove eel from the skewers and let cool before using in sushi. It can also be sliced and served with soy sauce and pickled ginger.

squid

Select only the freshest squid, or *ika*, for sushi. If purchasing whole squid, make sure that the eyes are bright black and the skin shiny.

To prepare whole squid, pull the head, tentacles and attached intestines from the tubelike body. Reserve the tentacles if making stuffed squid (page 134). Remove the translucent, quill-shaped piece of cartilage from the body and discard. If making stuffed squid, leave the body whole; otherwise, cut the body in half lengthwise.

Place the squid, skin side up, on a clean cutting board. Grasp the two triangular fins and pull upward, removing the fins and colored skin. Wipe the squid clean using a damp kitchen towel, removing any remaining skin. Slice into bite-sized pieces for hand-formed or scattered sushi.

fresh vegetables

Many people outside Japan think of sushi as being made only with raw fish and sticky rice. Fresh vegetables, however, are an important ingredient in sushi and are also used to make an artistic presentation. As for fish, the Japanese principle of freshness applies, since the vegetables are eaten raw or blanched, and should have optimum flavor and texture. When shopping for vegetables, make a special trip to the best produce market in your area.

Avocado, with its buttery, pale green flesh, is popular in all forms of sushi, especially when paired with salmon. Coating avocado slices in fresh lemon juice, though not done by Japanese chefs, is a good practice as it prevents them from turning brown.

Carrots and the large white radish called daikon are finely shredded using a Japanese vegetable slicer or are cut into attractive flower shapes for garnishes. Carrots are also sliced into fine or thick strips and used in vegetarian rolled sushi for their flavor, texture and color.

Other vegetables called for in this book include firm English (hothouse) cucumbers, pencil-thin asparagus spears, snowpeas (mange-tout) and young green beans. Butter lettuce leaves are used in some rolled sushi.

other essential ingredients

Bonito flakes These pale pink flakes, called *katsuo-bushi,* are shaved from blocks of dried, smoked and cured bonito. The flakes, with their subtle fish flavor and aroma, are an essential ingredient in the making of dashi, Japanese stock. They should be stored in an airtight container.

Daikon This large cylindrical white radish, up to 20 inches (50 cm) long and 3 inches (7.5 cm) in diameter, has a pungent flavor and is believed to aid digestion. Select a daikon that is firm and has unblemished smooth skin. Peel and then shred using a Japanese vegetable slicer or cut into matchsticks or decorative shapes. Soaking the prepared daikon in ice water for 10 minutes crisps it. Drain before using.

Deep-fried tofu skins These deep-fried slices of tofu are slit on one side or cut in half to form pouches. In Japan *abura-age* are known as "golden purses." They are also referred to as tofu pouches or tofu pockets. The skins should be soaked briefly in boiling water to remove excess oil. They are then filled with vinegared rice to make *inari-zushi* (page 130), or are cut into slivers for adding to soups or for topping scattered sushi.

Ginger Rhizomes of the ginger plant are peeled and grated in small amounts for use as an aromatic, pungent flavoring. When purchasing fresh ginger, select rhizomes that are firm and have smooth skin. Store in the refrigerator.

Kombu Also known as konbu, dried sea kelp is an essential ingredient in dashi and sushi rice, where it contributes a subtle taste of the sea. Select dark, thick pieces of kombu. Do not rinse them before using, as this will destroy the flavor; instead, wipe with a damp cloth to remove any white residue on the surface. Store in an airtight container.

Lotus root *Renkon,* used in scattered sushi, is the crunchy, white, honeycombed root of the lotus plant. When the root is cut crosswise into slices, each slice has a pattern resembling a flower. Lotus root is generally not available fresh, but is found canned or pickled in vinegar. It does not require further cooking.

Mirin Made from rice, mirin is a wine that imparts a pleasant sweetness to omelets (page 34) and other preparations. Known as sweet rice wine or sweet sake, mirin should be stored in a cool, dark place after opening. If it is unavailable, substitute 1 teaspoon white sugar for each 1 tablespoon mirin called for in a recipe.

Miso This thick fermented paste of soybeans and a grain such as rice is the foundation for Japanese soups. Many types of miso are available. Two of the most common types are brown miso and white miso. Brown miso, also called red miso, has a richer, saltier flavor than white miso, which is golden in color. Sold in plastic containers or packages, miso should be stored in an airtight container in the refrigerator.

Nori Dried tissue-thin sheets of this seaweed, sold in packages, are essential for preparing rolled sushi. Nori is also shredded and used as a garnish. The sheets need to be toasted briefly over an open flame or in a hot oven. Alternatively, you can purchase already toasted sheets, *yaki-nori*. The sheets should be cut with a sharp knife or kitchen scissors. Most measure 7 by 8 inches (18 by 20 cm). Store them in a sealed container in a dark place.

Pickled daikon radish Bright yellow in color, sections of pickled daikon, or *takuan,* are sold in packages. The daikon is finely sliced into matchsticks for rolled sushi.

Bonito flakes

Daikon

Deep-fried tofu skins

Fresh ginger

Kombu

Lotus root

...n, rice vinegar, sake, soy sauce and sushi vinegar

Miso

Nori

Pickled ginger (gari) Slices of fresh ginger are pickled with salt and vinegar, and generally colored pink. Eating a small amount cleanses the palate between mouthfuls of sushi and aids digestion. Opened containers of *gari* should be stored in the refrigerator. You can also make your own pickled ginger (page 36).

Rice vinegar This pale gold vinegar, called *su*, has a mild flavor ideally suited for flavoring the rice used in sushi.

Sake Japan's national alcoholic beverage, a mildly sweet wine made from fermented rice, can be enjoyed warm or chilled. It is also used in cooking. For this purpose, look for an inexpensive sake. Dry sherry may be substituted.

Sesame seeds These small black or tan seeds, which have an earthy, nutty taste, are an ingredient in sushi rolls and are used as a garnish. Lightly toasting them in a dry frying pan brings out their flavor.

Shiitake mushrooms Appreciated for their meaty texture and earthy flavor, both fresh and dried shiitakes are used in sushi. The fresh mushrooms need only be brushed clean and their tough stems removed. Dried shiitake should be reconstituted in hot water or dashi for 30 minutes, then drained and any thick woody stems removed. Store the dried mushrooms in an airtight container in a cool place.

Shiso leaf An aromatic herb belonging to the mint family, *shiso* has an alluring flavor that complements sushi, whether used as an ingredient in rolled sushi or as an edible garnish.

Soy sauce Made from fermented soybeans, wheat and salt, soy sauce, or *shoyu*, is an ingredient in cooking and serves as a dipping sauce for sushi and sashimi. For the best flavor, select Japanese soy sauce.

Sushi rice Japanese short-grain white rice is high in starch, which produces the characteristic sticky grains essential for making sushi. Be sure to use sushi rice; other varieties are not suitable.

Sushi vinegar This prepared mixture of rice vinegar, salt and sugar, sold in bottles, is mixed into steamed rice to make sushi rice. Do not use this commercial product in place of rice vinegar when making a vinegar mix for sushi rice.

Umeboshi plums A particular variety of small plum is preserved to make this sweet and salty pickle sold in jars or packages at Japanese markets. Before the pickle is used in sushi, the pits are removed and the flesh chopped. Once opened, containers of *umeboshi* should be stored in the refrigerator.

Wasabi

Fresh wasabi is also known as *namida*, meaning "tears," which helps explain the effect of eating this condiment made from the intensely hot rhizome of Japanese horseradish. True wasabi is very expensive and difficult to find outside Japan. All of the recipes in this book use what is known as wasabi powder or paste, a combination of wasabi, Chinese mustard and sometimes other types of horseradish. Powdered wasabi, sold in small tins, has a longer shelf life than wasabi paste. The powder needs to be reconstituted in water. Combine 1 teaspoon wasabi powder with $1/2$–1 teaspoon water and mix to form a stiff paste. Let stand for 5 minutes before using. Wasabi paste, sold in tubes, should be stored in the refrigerator after opening.

Pickled ginger (gari)

Pickled daikon radish

Sushi rice

Sesame seeds

Shiso leaf

Dried shiitake mushrooms

Umeboshi plums

Wasabi

basic techniques

how to make sushi rice

2 cups (14 oz/440 g) sushi rice
3 cups (24 fl oz/750 ml) water
1 piece kombu (optional)

1. Place rice in a colander and rinse under cold running water until water runs clear. Place rice, water and kombu (if using) in a heavy-bottomed saucepan. Bring to a boil over medium heat, stirring occasionally. Remove kombu.
2. Reduce heat to low, cover and simmer for 12 minutes. Do not lift lid while rice cooks.
3. Remove from heat and let stand, covered, for 10 minutes.

Note: When making $^1/_2$ recipe, cooking time remains 12 minutes.

how to prepare sushi vinegar

¼ cup (2 fl oz/60 ml) rice vinegar
2 tablespoons sugar
1 teaspoon salt

In a small glass or ceramic bowl, combine vinegar, sugar and salt. Stir until dissolved.

how to combine cooked rice and sushi vinegar

1. Place hot cooked rice in a wooden rice tub or large, shallow nonmetallic bowl. Using a rice paddle or wooden spoon, spread rice evenly in tub. Fold rice, using a cutting rather than stirring motion, to separate rice grains.
2. Make a shallow well in center of rice. While continuing to fold rice, sprinkle with sushi vinegar.
3. Continuing to fold rice with a cutting action, fan it with a hand-held or electric fan until rice cools to room temperature. Cover with a damp kitchen towel, then a lid. Do not refrigerate; rice will keep for 1 day.

27

how to slice fish fillets

Fillets for sushi and sashimi should have the skin and any errant bones removed. How a fillet is sliced depends on the type of sushi being prepared.

A piece of fresh salmon is used here to demonstrate the various methods, which can be applied to other types of fish. Remember that it is important to cut across the grain.

For **hand-rolled sushi** and **thick-rolled sushi**: Cut fillet into slices $\frac{1}{2}$ inch (12 mm) thick, $\frac{1}{2}$ inch (12 mm) wide and about 3 inches (7.5 cm) long. For **thin-rolled** sushi, cut into slices $\frac{1}{4}$ inch (6 mm) thick.

For **hand-formed sushi**: Cut fillet diagonally into slices $\frac{1}{4}$ inch (6 mm) thick, 1 inch (2.5 cm) wide and 2 inches (5 cm) long.

For **pressed sushi**: Cut fillet into slices about $\frac{1}{8}$ inch (3 mm) thick.

For **scattered sushi** and **sashimi**: Cut fillet into slices $\frac{1}{2}$ inch (12 mm) thick.

Hand-rolled

Hand-formed

Pressed

Scattered

29 basic techniques

how to prepare shrimp

Jumbo shrimp (king prawns), which are naturally curled, need to be cooked on bamboo skewers to make them straight. Take care not to overcook shrimp or they will turn tough and rubbery.

1. Holding a shrimp with legs facing upward, insert a wooden skewer under transparent shell, starting from where body joins head (do not insert skewer into shrimp head). Cook in a large saucepan of boiling salted water until flesh turns bright pink and white, 2–3 minutes. Drain and plunge in a bowl of iced water to halt cooking. Peel shrimp, leaving tail intact.

2. Using a sharp knife, cut along underside of each shrimp until you reach dark intestinal vein. Do not cut completely through shrimp. Remove vein with tip of knife. Briefly rinse shrimp under cold running water and pat dry with paper towels.

3. Using a knife or kitchen scissors, trim ends of shrimp tails, to neaten them.

how to make marinated mackerel

Marinated mackerel is a traditional Japanese dish. Salting the mackerel before marinating it in rice vinegar was originally a way to preserve the fish before refrigeration became common. The rice vinegar enhances the flavor of the mackerel's oily flesh. Marinated mackerel can be sliced and arranged on a plate with your choice of decoration or can be used for pressed sushi (page 124), hand-formed sushi or rolled sushi.

2 mackerel fillets, about 5 oz (150 g) each
sea salt
rice vinegar

1. Place mackerel fillets in a large glass or ceramic bowl and sprinkle liberally with salt. Rub salt into fillets, coating them evenly. Transfer to a colander, place colander over a bowl and let stand for 1 hour.
2. Rinse fish under cold running water to remove salt. Pat dry with paper towels.
3. Place fish in a clean, shallow glass or ceramic dish. Pour in rice vinegar to cover. Set aside to marinate for 1 hour. Drain and pat dry with paper towels. Flesh should have turned whiter.
4. Place on a wooden board and use tweezers to remove any bones. Enclose fillets in plastic wrap and refrigerate until serving.

how to make an omelet

A square or rectangular frying pan is traditionally used for making Japanese omelets, or *tamago yaki*. You can substitute an 8-inch (20-cm) round frying pan, then trim the cooked omelet into a square or rectangle. The cooked omelet will keep for 1 day, enclosed in plastic wrap and stored in the refrigerator. It can be sliced as a topping for hand-formed sushi or as a filling for rolled sushi. Slices can also be added to a bowl of scattered sushi.

6 eggs, beaten
½ cup (4 fl oz/125 ml) dashi (see page 142)
2 tablespoons sugar
1 teaspoon salt
1 tablespoon sake
1 tablespoon mirin
1 tablespoon canola oil

1. In a bowl, combine eggs, dashi, sugar, salt, sake and mirin. Stir with a fork until well combined.

2. In frying pan over medium heat, warm oil. Using chopsticks and a paper towel, wipe excess oil from pan. Set paper towel aside.

3. Pour one-third of egg mixture in pan to cover bottom. Cook until surface begins to set. Loosen omelet from surface of pan with a spatula. Using chopsticks or a fork, fold cooked omelet toward you in fourths, then push to far end of pan, away from you.

4. Coat exposed pan surface with oil on reserved towel. Add another third of egg mixture and gently lift folded omelet to allow egg mixture to cover bottom of pan. Cook until surface begins to set. Loosen omelet from pan surface with a spatula. Again using chopsticks or fork, fold cooked omelet toward you in fourths, folding it over first cooked omelet. Push to far end of pan, away from you.

5. Coat exposed pan surface with oil on reserved towel. Add remaining egg mixture to pan and gently lift folded omelets to allow egg mixture to cover bottom of pan. Cook until surface begins to set. Loosen omelet from pan surface with a spatula. Again using chopsticks or fork, fold cooked omelet toward you, folding it over previously cooked omelets.

6. Slide onto a bamboo mat and roll up tightly. This helps form folded omelets into a rectangular shape. Let cool completely, then remove bamboo mat.

7. Slice omelet as directed in individual recipes.

Makes 20–30 slices

how to make pickled ginger

Pickled ginger, or *gari,* is a traditional accompaniment to sushi and sashimi. It is sold in jars, but you can prepare your own. If you prefer to leave out the food coloring, you can add a slice of uncooked beet, which will give the ginger a pretty pink color.

10 oz (300 g) fresh root ginger, peeled
2 tablespoons sea salt
1 cup (8 fl oz/250 ml) rice vinegar
7 oz (220 g) sugar
½ cup (4 fl oz/125 ml) water
1 or 2 drops red food coloring

1. Cut ginger crosswise into very thin slices using a Japanese vegetable slicer or a vegetable peeler. Place in a colander and sprinkle with sea salt. Let stand for 1 hour. Rinse ginger under cold running water to remove salt.
2. Place vinegar, sugar and water in a saucepan. Bring to a boil over high heat, stirring until sugar dissolves. Boil for 5 minutes, remove from heat and let cool. Add food coloring.
3. Place ginger slices in a sterilized jar and add cooled vinegar mixture. Seal jar and refrigerate for 1 week before using.

decorations

In Japan a plate of sushi or sashimi is traditionally garnished with beautiful decorations, making the final presentation a work of art. Decorations can be as elaborate as the carved bamboo leaves made by Japanese master chefs after many years of practice, or they can be simple enough to be created by a home cook. When deciding which decorations to use, choose those that complement the color and texture of the ingredients in the sushi being served. Here are some basic but elegant garnishes that will transform all of your sushi plates into masterpieces.

Shredded nori Fold a sheet of toasted nori in half. Using sharp scissors, cut into very fine strips. Divide into 4 batches. Place each batch in the palm of one hand, then use both hands to roll strips into a rough ball, compacting nori with your fingertips to crease it. Then gently pull strips from the ball to create an attractive shape.

Shredded carrot Peel a carrot, then finely shred using a Japanese vegetable slicer. Place in a bowl of ice water for 10 minutes. Drain and place on kitchen towels to absorb excess moisture.

Camellia leaf Select fresh young leaves, rinse with cold water and dry before use. The leaves are available from florists or a home garden. They should not be eaten.

Fish rose Use tuna, salmon or white-fleshed fish such as sea bream. Cut into slices measuring 1 inch (2.5 cm) by 3 inches (7.5 cm) by $1/4$ inch (6 mm) thick. Allow 2 slices per rose. Very tightly roll a slice to make center of rose, then roll another slice around center to make petals. Trim away any excess fish.

Bamboo leaves These green plastic leaves, available in Japanese supermarkets, are made to resemble carved bamboo leaves. They can be rinsed and reused.

Plastic fish soy sauce bottles These whimsical containers make a fun addition to a sushi party or a convenient way to carry soy sauce on a sushi picnic. They are sold in Japanese markets.

Carrot flower Peel a carrot. Cut into thin slices for decoration, thicker slices for scattered sushi (page 116). Using a metal flower cutter (available in Japanese markets), cut a flower from each slice. Alternatively, cut out with a small flower cookie cutter.

Shiso leaf These aromatic leaves make excellent edible garnishes. Before using the leaves, refresh in cold water, then pat dry with a kitchen towel.

Shredded daikon Peel daikon, then finely shred using a Japanese vegetable slicer. Place in a bowl of ice water for 10 minutes. Drain and place on kitchen towels to absorb excess moisture.

Cucumber pine branch Begin with a 2-inch (5-cm) section of English (hothouse) cucumber. Cut in half. You should have 2 semicircular pieces with skin on curved sides. Cut off curved side of each semicircle to form 2 rectangles. Working with 1 rectangle at a time, cut an odd number of slices along rectangle, each about $1/8$ inch (3 mm) wide and $1 1/2$ inches (4 cm) long, leaving the final $1/2$ inch (12 mm) uncut. Using your fingers, carefully fold every second slice into the gap between itself and the next slice.

Wasabi leaf In a small bowl, mix 2 tablespoons wasabi powder with a little cold water to form a stiff paste. Let stand for 2 minutes. Roll paste with your fingers to form a cylinder. Place on a chopping board and pinch one end to make a stem. Moisten a knife blade and use it to flatten cylinder. Form into a leaf shape with your fingertips. Smooth over any cracks with knife blade. With tip of knife, score veins on leaf. Cover with plastic wrap to keep moist until serving. Use soon after making as strength of wasabi diminishes quickly.

Pickled ginger flower Select longest slices of pickled ginger and drain. Very tightly roll a slice for center of rose, then roll additional slices around center, one at a time, to make more petals.

sashimi

Sashimi is a dish consisting of raw fish fillets cut into bite-sized pieces, eaten with soy sauce and wasabi. It is traditionally regarded as the perfect start to a Japanese meal.

Many types of raw fish can be used for sashimi, the most common being tuna, yellowtail, mackerel, salmon, sea bream and flounder. Shellfish such as shrimp (prawns), lobster, abalone and crab are also used. It is important that the seafood be impeccably fresh. Fishmongers may offer to slice the fish for you, but it is best to do this at home just prior to serving. As a guide, allow $1/4$ lb (125 g) per person.

classic sashimi

8 oz (250 g) sashimi-grade salmon
8 oz (250 g) sashimi-grade tuna
decorations (pages 38–41)
Japanese soy sauce for serving
wasabi for serving

1. Cut salmon and tuna into slices about $1/2$ inch (12 mm) thick.
2. Arrange on serving plates with your choice of decorations. Serve with soy sauce and wasabi.

Serves 4

tuna and nori rolls

2 sheets toasted nori, quartered

8 pieces sashimi-quality tuna, each 1 inch
   (2.5 cm) thick x 1 inch (2.5 cm) wide x 3 inches
   (7.5 cm) long

wasabi

Japanese soy sauce for serving

1. Place a piece of nori, shiny side down, on a dry chopping board.
2. Arrange a piece of tuna along center of nori.
3. Spread a little wasabi along tuna.
4. Roll nori around tuna. Cut roll into 3 equal pieces. Repeat with remaining nori and tuna. Serve with soy sauce.

Makes 24 pieces

Variation: Replace tuna with same quantity of sashimi-quality salmon.

thin-rolled sushi (hosomaki-zushi)

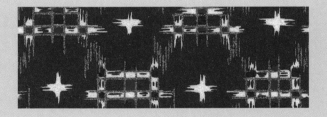

cucumber thin rolls

Thin-rolled sushi, or *hosomaki-zushi*, is the simplest sushi. It generally uses a single filling in addition to rice. If you are new to making sushi, begin with this style, so you can master the technique of rolling nori to contain a filling. Cut into bite-sized pieces, the slim rolls make excellent finger food for parties, snacks, lunches and picnics.

3 sheets toasted nori, halved lengthwise
½ recipe sushi rice (pages 26–27)
½ English (hothouse) cucumber, skin intact, seeds
removed, cut into strips ¼ inch (6 mm) thick x
¼ inch (6 mm) wide x 3 inches (7.5 cm) long

1. Place 1 half sheet of nori, shiny side down, horizontally on a bamboo rolling mat. Wet your hands and pick up a ball of rice slightly smaller than than a golf-ball. Gently squeeze rice into an oblong shape and put in center of nori sheet. Spread rice evenly over nori, leaving a $^3/_4$-inch (2-cm) strip uncovered along edge farthest from you.

2. Arrange 2 cucumber strips along center of rice, lining them up together without leaving any gaps. Set your fingers on cucumber strips to hold them in place, lift up edge of mat closest to you and roll mat away from you, evenly and gently pressing on cucumber to keep roll firm.

3. Continue to roll mat forward and arrange roll seam side down, applying gentle pressure. Moisture of sticky rice will seal roll. Use mat to shape roll into a round or square log (a square shape is traditional). Remove mat. Cut roll in half crosswise, then cut each half into 3 equal pieces. Repeat with remaining ingredients.

Makes 36 pieces

Variation: Sprinkle sushi rice with 2 teaspoons toasted sesame seeds before rolling.

salmon thin rolls (pictured)

3 sheets toasted nori, halved lengthwise
½ recipe sushi rice (pages 26–27)
wasabi
12 strips sashimi-grade salmon, each ¼ inch
  (6 mm) thick x ¼ inch (6 mm) wide x 3 inches
  (7.5 cm) long
Japanese soy sauce for serving

Follow method for preparing cucumber rolls (page 50), spreading wasabi over rice and using 2 salmon strips for each half sheet of nori. Serve with soy sauce.

Makes 36 pieces

egg thin rolls

3 sheets toasted nori, halved lengthwise
½ recipe sushi rice (pages 26-27)
6 teaspoons mayonnaise
12 strips of omelet (page 34), each
  ¼ inch (6 mm) thick x ¼ inch (6 mm) wide x
  3 inches (7.5 cm) long
pickled ginger for serving
Japanese soy sauce for serving

Follow method for preparing cucumber rolls (page 50), spreading mayonnaise over rice and using 2 omelet strips for each half sheet of nori. Serve with pickled ginger and soy sauce.

Makes 36 pieces

deluxe pickled radish flower

3 sheets toasted nori, halved lengthwise
½ recipe sushi rice (page 26–27)
6 oz (180 g) drained pickled radish, cut into thin
matchsticks
Japanese soy sauce for serving

1. Place 1 half sheet of nori, shiny side down, horizontally on a bamboo rolling mat. Wet your hands and pick up a ball of rice slightly smaller than a golf ball. Gently squeeze rice into an oblong shape and put in center of nori sheet. Spread rice evenly over nori, leaving a $^3/_4$-inch (2-cm) strip uncovered along edge farthest from you.

2. Arrange one-sixth of pickled daikon along center of rice, lining them up together without leaving any gaps. Set your fingers on daikon strips to hold them in place, lift up edge of mat closest to you and roll mat away from you, evenly and gently pressing on daikon to keep roll firm.

3. Continue to roll mat forward and arrange roll seam side down, applying gentle pressure. Moisture of sticky rice will seal roll. Use mat to shape roll into a petal shape.

4. Remove bamboo mat. Cut roll in half crosswise, then cut each half into 3 equal pieces. You will have 6 petal-shaped sushi. Repeat with remaining ingredients.

5. Arrange 6 pieces on each serving plate with points facing center to make a flower. Serve with soy sauce.

Makes 36 pieces

plum and shiso leaf thin rolls

3 sheets toasted nori, halved lengthwise
½ recipe sushi rice (page 26–27)
30 umeboshi plums, pitted and chopped
4 shiso leaves, finely shredded
Japanese soy sauce for serving

1. Place 1 half sheet of nori, shiny side down, horizontally on a bamboo rolling mat. Wet your hands and pick up a ball of rice slightly smaller than a golf ball. Gently squeeze rice into an oblong shape and put in center of nori sheet. Spread rice evenly over nori, leaving a $^3/_4$-inch (2-cm) strip uncovered along edge farthest from you.

2. Arrange one-sixth of chopped umeboshi plums and one-sixth of shredded shiso along center of rice, without leaving any gaps. Set your fingers on filling ingredients to hold them in place, lift up edge of mat closest to you and roll mat away from you, evenly and gently pressing on filling to keep roll firm.

3. Continue to roll mat forward and arrange roll seam side down, applying gentle pressure. Moisture of sticky rice will seal roll. Use mat to shape roll into a round or square log.

4. Remove bamboo mat. Cut roll in half crosswise, then cut each half into 3 equal pieces. Repeat with remaining ingredients.

5. Serve with soy sauce.

Makes 36 pieces

bento box – japanese lunch box

In Japan, lunches and dinners are beautifully packaged in bento boxes made of wood and finished with red lacquer. Nowadays, some are plastic. The boxes have compartments to hold a selection of sushi and/or rice, fish, vegetables and pickles. Each box comes with chopsticks and a tiny bottle of soy sauce. The meals are sold at bus and train stations throughout Japan. They are the ultimate street food. The boxes can be purchased from Japanese specialty stores and can also be used to serve sushi at the table.

Pictured opposite is a selection of thin rolls (hosomaki) including Tuna thin rolls, Cucumber thin rolls and Salmon thin rolls.

tuna thin rolls

3 sheets toasted nori, halved lengthwise
½ recipe sushi rice (page 26–27)
wasabi
12 strips sashimi-quality tuna, each ¼ inch
  (6 mm) thick x ¼ inch (6 mm) wide x 3 inches
  (7.5 cm) long
Japanese soy sauce for serving

Follow method for preparing cucumber rolls (page 50), spreading wasabi over rice and using 2 tuna strips for each half sheet of nori. Serve with soy sauce.

Makes 36 pieces

asparagus and wasabi thin rolls

18 thin asparagus spears
3 sheets toasted nori, halved lengthwise
½ recipe sushi rice (pages 26–27)
wasabi
Japanese soy sauce for serving

Bring a saucepan of water to a boil. Snap off tough ends from asparagus spears, then cut each in half lengthwise. Plunge asparagus pieces in boiling water and cook for 1 minute. Drain asparagus and refresh in a bowl of ice water. Drain again and let cool completely.

Follow method for preparing cucumber rolls (page 50), spreading wasabi over rice and using 3 asparagus pieces for each half sheet of nori. Serve with soy sauce.

Makes 36 pieces

carrot thin rolls

Follow method for preparing cucumber rolls (page 50), spreading mayonnaise over rice and using 2 carrot strips for each half sheet of nori. Serve with soy sauce.

Makes 36 pieces

3 sheets toasted nori, halved lengthwise
½ recipe sushi rice (pages 26–27)
6 teaspoons mayonnaise
6 oz (180 g) carrot, peeled and cut into strips
¼ inch (6 mm) thick x ¼ inch (6 mm)
wide x 3 inches (7.5 cm) long
Japanese soy for serving

thick-rolled sushi (futomaki-zushi)

salmon and avocado thick rolls

The technique for making thick rolls is similar to that for thin-rolled sushi. The difference is that thick-rolled sushi, or *futomaki-zushi*, generally uses multiple filling ingredients and a full sheet of nori.

4 sheets toasted nori
1 recipe sushi rice (pages 26–27)
wasabi
½ avocado, peeled, pitted and thinly sliced
12 strips sashimi-quality salmon, each ½ inch
   (12 mm) thick x ½ inch (12 mm) wide x 3 inches
   (7.5 cm) long
pickled ginger for serving
Japanese soy sauce for serving

1. Place 1 sheet of nori, shiny side down, horizontally on a bamboo rolling mat. Wet your hands and pick up about $^3/_4$ cup of sushi rice. Gently squeeze rice into an oblong shape and put in center of nori sheet. Spread rice evenly over nori, leaving a $^3/_4$-inch (2-cm) strip uncovered along edge farthest from you.

2. Using a finger, take a dab of wasabi and wipe across center of rice. Arrange one-fourth of avocado slices and 3 salmon strips along center of rice, lining them up together without leaving any gaps. Set your fingers on ingredients to hold them in place, lift up edge of mat closest to you and slowly roll mat away from you, evenly and gently pressing on filling to keep roll firm.

3. Continue to roll mat forward and arrange roll seam side down, applying gentle pressure. Moisture of sticky rice will help seal roll. Use mat to shape roll into a round or square log.

4. Remove bamboo mat. Using dry hands, gently reshape if necessary. Cut roll in half crosswise, then cut each half into 4 equal pieces. Repeat with remaining ingredients. Serve with pickled ginger and soy sauce.

Makes 32 pieces

1

2

3

4

65

tuna and lettuce thick rolls

1 can (13 oz/400 g) tuna in water, drained
2 tablespoons mayonnaise
1 teaspoon wasabi paste (optional)
4 sheets toasted nori
1 recipe sushi rice (pages 26–27)
6 butter (Boston) lettuce leaves, torn
Japanese soy sauce for serving

1. Place tuna in a bowl and mash with a fork. Add mayonnaise and wasabi (if using) and mix until well combined.

2. Place 1 sheet of nori, shiny side down, horizontally onto a bamboo rolling mat. Wet your hands and pick up about $^{3}/_{4}$ cup of sushi rice. Gently squeeze rice into an oblong shape and put in center of nori sheet. Spread rice evenly over nori, leaving a $^{3}/_{4}$-inch (2-cm) strip uncovered along edge farthest from you.

3. Spoon one-fourth of tuna mixture along center of rice. Arrange one-fourth of lettuce over tuna without leaving any gaps. Set your fingers on ingredients to hold them in place, lift up edge of mat closest to you and slowly roll mat away from you, evenly and gently pressing on filling to keep roll firm.

4. Continue to roll mat forward and arrange roll seam side down, applying gentle pressure. Moisture of sticky rice will help seal roll. Use mat to shape roll into a round or square log.

5. Remove bamboo mat. Using dry hands, gently reshape roll if necessary. Cut roll in half crosswise, then cut each half into 4 equal pieces. Repeat with remaining ingredients. Serve with soy sauce.

Makes 32 pieces

pickled radish and cucumber thick rolls

4 sheets toasted nori

1 recipe sushi rice (pages 26–27)

7 oz (220 g) pickled radish, drained and cut into thin matchstick lengths

½ English (hothouse) cucumber, skin intact, seeds removed, cut into strips ¼ inch (6 mm) thick x ¼ inch (6 mm) wide x 3 inches (7.5 cm) long

pickled ginger for serving

Japanese soy for serving

Follow method for preparing salmon and avocado thick rolls (page 64), using pickled daikon and cucumber in place of wasabi, salmon and avocado. Serve with pickled ginger and soy sauce.

Makes 32 pieces

vegetarian thick rolls

4 sheets toasted nori

1 recipe sushi rice (pages 26–27)

8 oz (250 g) carrots, peeled and cut into thin matchsticks

½ avocado, peeled, pitted and thinly sliced

pickled ginger for serving

Japanese soy sauce for serving

Follow method for preparing salmon and avocado thick rolls (page 64), using carrots in place of wasabi and salmon. Arrange avocado on top of carrots. Serve with pickled ginger and soy sauce.

Makes 32 pieces

california thick rolls

4 sheets toasted nori
1 recipe sushi rice (pages 26–27)
8 teaspoons flying fish roe
1 small avocado, peeled, pitted and thinly sliced
½ cucumber, skin intact, seeds removed, cut into
long, thin lengths
8 jumbo shrimp (king prawns), cooked (page 30)
and tails removed
Japanese soy sauce for serving

1. Place a sheet of nori, shiny side down, horizontally on a bamboo rolling mat. Wet your hands and pick up about $3/4$ cup of sushi rice. Gently squeeze rice into an oblong shape and put in center of nori sheet. Spread rice evenly over nori, leaving about a $3/4$-inch (2-cm) strip uncovered along edge farthest from you.

2. Spread one-fourth of flying fish roe along center of rice. Arrange one-fourth of avocado slices and cucumber strips along center of rice, lining them up together without leaving any gaps. Finally, arrange shrimp over avocado and cucumber. Set your fingers on ingredients to hold them in place, lift up edge of mat closest to you and slowly roll mat away from you, evenly and gently pressing on filling to keep roll firm.

3. Continue to roll mat forward and arrange roll seam side down, applying gentle pressure. Moisture of sticky rice will help seal roll. Use mat to shape roll into a round or square log.

4. Remove bamboo mat. Using dry hands, gently reshape if necessary. Cut roll in half crosswise, then cut each half into 4 equal pieces. Repeat with remaining ingredients. Serve with soy sauce.

Makes 32 pieces

Variation: Substitute 1 can (14 oz/425 g) crabmeat for shrimp, and arrange $1/4$ of crabmeat over avocado and cucumber.

tempura shrimp thick rolls

FOR TEMPURA SHRIMP
8 jumbo shrimp (king prawns), peeled and deveined,
** tails intact**
2 cups (16 fl oz/500 ml) canola oil for deep-frying
1 egg, separated
1 tablespoon lemon juice
2/3 cup (5 fl oz/150 ml) cold water
1/3 cup (1 1/2 oz/45 g) all-purpose (plain) flour
pinch salt

4 sheets toasted nori
1 recipe sushi rice (pages 26–27)
4 teaspoons mayonnaise
1 teaspoon wasabi
4 butter (Boston) lettuce leaves, torn in half
Japanese soy sauce for serving

1. To make tempura shrimp, thread each shrimp on a bamboo skewer, making sure it is as straight as possible. Pat shrimp dry with paper towels.

2. In a saucepan or wok, heat oil until it reaches 375°F (190°C) on a deep-frying thermometer. A small cube of bread dropped in hot oil should sizzle and turn golden in 1 minute.

3. In a bowl, using a whisk or fork, mix together egg yolk, lemon juice and cold water. Add flour and salt and mix until smooth.

4. In a bowl, using a whisk or electric mixer, beat egg white until soft peaks form. Using a spatula, fold egg white into batter.

5. Dip each shrimp in batter, then deep-fry in hot oil until golden, about 2 minutes. Transfer to paper towels to drain. Remove shrimp from skewers.

6. Place 1 sheet of nori, shiny side down, horizontally on a bamboo rolling mat. Wet your hands and pick up about 3/4 cup of sushi rice. Gently squeeze rice into an oblong shape and put in center of nori sheet. Spread rice evenly over nori, leaving a 3/4-inch (2-cm) strip uncovered along edge farthest from you.

7. In a small bowl, combine mayonnaise and wasabi. Spoon one-fourth of wasabi mixture across center of rice. Arrange one-fourth of lettuce and 2 tempura shrimp along center of rice, orienting shrimp so tails face outward. Set your fingers on ingredients to hold them in place, lift up edge of mat closest to you and slowly roll mat away from you, evenly and gently pressing on filling to keep roll firm.

8. Continue to roll mat forward and arrange roll seam side down, applying gentle pressure. Moisture of sticky rice will help seal roll. Use mat to shape roll into a round or square log.

9. Remove bamboo mat. Using dry hands, gently reshape roll if necessary. Cut roll in half crosswise. If desired, cut each half into 4 equal pieces, making a total of 32 pieces. Repeat with remaining ingredients. Serve with soy sauce.

Makes 8 rolls

omelet and cucumber thick rolls

4 sheets toasted nori

1 recipe sushi rice (pages 26–27)

8 teaspoons mayonnaise

4 slices omelet (page 34), each ½ inch (12 mm) thick x ½ inch (12 mm) wide x 3 inches (7.5 cm) long

½ English (hothouse) cucumber, skin intact, seeds removed, cut into strips ¼ inch (6 mm) thick x ¼ inch (6 mm wide) x 3 inches (7.5 cm) long

Japanese soy sauce for serving

Follow method for preparing salmon and avocado thick rolls (page 64), using mayonnaise in place of wasabi, and omelet slices and cucumber strips in place of salmon and avocado. Serve with soy sauce.

Makes 32 pieces

Inside-outside sushi rolls (uramaki-zushi)

california inside-outside rolls

Making inside-outside rolls, called *uramaki*, is easier than it looks—even easier than assembling traditional thick rolls (*futomaki-zushi)*. The bamboo rolling mat is first covered with plastic wrap to prevent the sushi rice from sticking to it. The rice is spread over the entire sheet of nori, then the sheet is turned over before rolling. The finished roll has rice both inside and outside.

2 sheets toasted nori, halved lengthwise
½ recipe sushi rice (pages 26–27)
4 tablespoons flying fish roe
½ avocado, peeled, pitted and thinly sliced
½ English (hothouse) cucumber, skin intact, seeds
  removed, cut into long thin lengths
8 jumbo shrimp (king prawns), cooked (page 30)
  and tails removed
Japanese soy sauce for serving
wasabi for serving

1. Cover a bamboo rolling mat with 2 large pieces of plastic wrap, folding them over edges and overlapping them at back of mat. Place 1 half sheet of nori, shiny side down, horizontally on prepared mat. Wet your hands and pick up a ball of rice slightly larger than a golf ball. Gently squeeze rice into an oblong shape and put in center of nori sheet. Spread rice evenly over entire sheet up to edges.

2. Evenly spread rice with 1 tablespoon flying fish roe. Pick up rice-covered nori by corners and quickly turn over so rice side is facing down.

3. Arrange one-fourth of avocado slices and cucumber strips along center of rice, lining them up together without leaving any gaps. Arrange 2 shrimp over avocado and cucumber. Set your fingers on ingredients to hold them in place, lift up edge of mat closest to you and slowly roll mat away from you, evenly and gently pressing on filling to keep roll firm.

4. Continue to roll mat forward and arrange roll seam side down, applying gentle pressure. Moisture of sticky rice will help seal roll. Use mat to shape roll into a round or square log. Remove bamboo mat. Cut roll in half crosswise, then cut each half into 3 equal pieces. Repeat with remaining ingredients. Serve with soy sauce and wasabi.

Makes 24 pieces

Variation: Substitute 10 oz/300 g canned (drained) or fresh crabmeat for shrimp, and arrange ¼ of crabmeat over avocado and cucumber.

1

2

3

4

79

eel and cucumber inside-outside rolls

2 sheets toasted nori, halved lengthwise

½ recipe sushi rice (pages 26–27)

2 tablespoons black sesame seeds

½ English (hothouse) cucumber, skin intact, seeds removed, cut into strips ¼ inch (6 mm) thick x ¼ inch (6 mm) wide x 3 inches (7.5 cm) long

8 strips cooked eel (page 18), each ½ inch (12 mm) thick x ½ inch (12 mm) wide x 3 inches (7.5 cm) long

Japanese soy sauce for serving

1. Cover a bamboo rolling mat with 2 large pieces of plastic wrap, folding them over edges and overlapping them at back of mat. Place 1 half sheet of nori, shiny side down, horizontally on prepared mat. Wet your hands and pick up a ball of rice slightly larger than a golf ball. Gently squeeze rice into an oblong shape and put in center of nori sheet. Spread rice evenly over entire sheet up to edges.

2. Evenly sprinkle rice with 2 teaspoons sesame seeds. Pick up rice-covered nori by corners and quickly turn over so rice side is facing down.

3. Arrange one-fourth of cucumber strips and 2 eel strips along center of rice, lining them up together without leaving any gaps. Set your fingers on ingredients to hold them in place, lift up edge of mat closest to you and slowly roll mat away from you, evenly and gently pressing on filling to keep roll firm.

4. Continue to roll mat forward and arrange roll seam side down, applying gentle pressure. Moisture of sticky rice will help seal roll. Use mat to shape roll into a round or square log. Remove bamboo mat. Cut roll in half crosswise, then cut each half into 3 equal pieces. Repeat with remaining ingredients. Serve with soy sauce.

Makes 24 pieces

salmon and avocado inside-outside rolls

2 sheets toasted nori, halved lengthwise
½ recipe sushi rice (pages 26–27)
4 tablespoons flying fish roe
wasabi
1 small avocado, peeled, pitted and thinly sliced
½ English (hothouse) cucumber, skin and seeds
   removed, cut into long, thin lengths
8 strips sashimi-quality salmon, each ¼ inch
   (6 mm) thick x ¼ inch (6 mm) wide x 3 inches
   (7.5 cm) long
Japanese soy sauce for serving
pickled ginger for serving

1. Cover a bamboo rolling mat with 2 large pieces of plastic wrap, folding them over edges and overlapping them at back of mat. Place 1 half sheet of nori, shiny side down, horizontally on prepared mat. Wet your hands and pick up a ball of rice slightly larger than a golf ball. Gently squeeze rice into an oblong shape and put in center of nori sheet. Spread rice evenly over entire sheet up to edges.

2. Evenly spread rice with 1 tablespoon flying fish roe. Pick up rice-covered nori by corners and quickly turn over so rice side is facing down.

3. Spread a little wasabi across center of nori. Arrange one-fourth of avocado slices, cucumber strips and salmon strips along center of rice, lining them up together without leaving any gaps. Set your fingers on ingredients to hold them in place, lift up edge of mat closest to you and slowly roll mat away from you, evenly and gently pressing on filling to keep roll firm.

4. Continue to roll mat forward and arrange roll seam side down, applying gentle pressure. Moisture of sticky rice will help seal roll. Use mat to shape roll into a round or square log. Remove bamboo mat. Cut roll in half crosswise, then cut each half into 3 equal pieces. Repeat with remaining ingredients. Serve with soy sauce and pickled ginger.

Makes 24 pieces

vegetarian inside-outside rolls

2 sheets toasted nori, halved lengthwise

½ recipe sushi rice (pages 26–27)

8 teaspoons sesame seeds, toasted

4 teaspoons mayonnaise

6 oz (180 g) carrot, peeled and cut into matchsticks

½ English (hothouse) cucumber, skin intact, seeds
   removed, cut into long, thin lengths

4 scallions (shallots/spring onions), white and pale
   green parts, cut into long, thin lengths

Japanese soy sauce for serving

wasabi for serving

pickled ginger for serving

1. Cover a bamboo rolling mat with 2 large pieces of plastic wrap, folding them over edges and overlapping them at back of mat. Place 1 half sheet of nori, shiny side down, horizontally on prepared mat. Wet your hands and pick up a ball of rice slightly larger than a golf ball. Gently squeeze rice into an oblong shape and put in center of nori sheet. Spread rice evenly over entire sheet up to edges.

2. Evenly sprinkle rice with about 2 teaspoons sesame seeds. Pick up rice-covered nori by corners and quickly turn over so rice side is facing down.

3. Spread 1 teaspoon mayonnaise across center of nori. Arrange one-fourth of carrot strips, cucumber strips and scallions along center of rice, lining them up together without leaving any gaps. Set your fingers on ingredients to hold them in place, lift up edge of mat closest to you and slowly roll mat away from you, evenly and gently pressing on filling to keep roll firm.

4. Continue to roll mat forward and arrange roll seam side down, applying gentle pressure. Moisture of sticky rice will help seal roll. Use mat to shape roll into a round or square log. Remove bamboo mat. Cut roll in half crosswise, then cut each half into 3 equal pieces. Repeat with remaining ingredients. Serve with soy sauce, wasabi and pickled ginger.

Makes 24 pieces

hand-rolled sushi (temaki-zushi)

tuna and cucumber hand rolls

Hand-rolled sushi, or *temaki-zushi*, is one of the easiest sushi to prepare. You can present a platter of fresh ingredients, a bowl of sushi rice and cut nori sheets, and let your family and friends roll their own.

6 sheets toasted nori, halved lengthwise
½ recipe sushi rice (pages 26–27)
wasabi
12 strips sashimi-quality tuna, each ½ inch (12 mm) thick x ½ inch (12 mm) wide x 3 inches (7.5 cm) long
12 strips English (hothouse) cucumber, each ½ inch (12 mm) thick x ½ inch (12 mm) wide x 3 inches (7.5 cm) long
Japanese soy sauce for serving

1. Place 1 half sheet of nori, shiny side down, in palm of one hand. Wet your other hand and place 2 heaping tablespoons sushi rice on left side of nori. Using wet fingertips, spread rice, flattening it with your fingers. Spread a little wasabi over rice.
2. Arrange 1 tuna strip and 1 cucumber strip diagonally over rice from center to outer left corner of nori.
3. Fold bottom left corner of nori toward top right corner, wrapping it around filling.
4. Roll nori into a cone shape. Adhere seam of cone with 2 or 3 grains of sushi rice and press to seal. Serve with soy sauce.

Makes 12

1

2

3

4

89

california hand rolls

6 sheets toasted nori, halved lengthwise
½ recipe sushi rice (pages 26–27)
½ avocado, peeled, pitted and thinly sliced
½ English (hothouse) cucumber, skin intact, seeds removed, cut into long, thin lengths
12 jumbo shrimp (king prawns), cooked (page 30) and tails removed
12 teaspoons flying fish roe
Japanese soy sauce for serving

1. Place 1 half sheet of nori, shiny side down, in palm of one hand. Wet your other hand and place 2 heaping tablespoons sushi rice on left side of nori. Using wet fingertips, spread rice, flattening it with your fingers.
2. Arrange 1 avocado slice, 2 or 3 lengths of cucumber and 1 shrimp diagonally over rice from center to outer left corner of nori. Spoon 1 teaspoon flying fish roe near top left corner of nori.
3. Fold bottom left corner of nori toward top right corner, wrapping it around filling
4. Roll nori into a cone shape. Adhere seam of cone with 2 or 3 grains of sushi rice and press to seal. Serve with soy sauce.

Makes 12

Variation: Substitute 1 can (14 oz/425 g) crabmeat for shrimp, and spoon $1/12$ of crabmeat diagonally over rice from center to outer left corner of nori.

tempura vegetable hand rolls

FOR TEMPURA VEGETABLES

1 carrot, peeled

1 zucchini (courgette), peel intact

2 cups (16 fl oz/500 ml) canola oil for deep-frying

1 egg, separated

1 tablespoon lemon juice

2/3 cup (5 fl oz/150 ml) cold water

1/3 cup (2 oz/60 g) all-purpose (plain) flour

pinch salt

6 sheets toasted nori, halved lengthwise

1/2 recipe sushi rice (pages 26–27)

6 teaspoons mayonnaise

3 butter (Boston) lettuce leaves, each torn into 4 pieces

Japanese soy sauce for serving

1. To make tempura vegetables, cut carrot and zucchini into strips 1/4 inch (6 mm) thick x 1/4 inch (6 mm) wide x 3 inches (7.5 cm) long. Pat vegetables dry with paper towels.

2. In a saucepan or wok, heat oil until it reaches 375°F (190°C) on a deep-frying thermometer. A small cube of bread dropped in hot oil should sizzle and turn golden in 1 minute.

3. In a bowl, using a whisk or fork, mix together egg yolk, lemon juice and cold water. Add flour and salt and mix until smooth.

4. In a bowl, using a whisk or electric mixer, beat egg white until soft peaks form. Using a spatula, fold egg white into batter.

5. Working in batches, dip carrot and zucchini strips in batter, then deep-fry in hot oil until golden, 1–2 minutes. Using a slotted spoon, transfer to paper towels to drain.

6. Place 1 half sheet of nori, shiny side down, in palm of one hand. Wet your other hand and place 2 heaping tablespoons sushi rice on left side of nori. Using wet fingertips, spread rice, flattening it with your fingers. Spread 1/2 teaspoon mayonnaise over rice.

7. Arrange 1 piece of lettuce and 2 or 3 tempura vegetables diagonally over rice from center to outer left corner of nori.

8. Fold bottom left corner of nori toward top right corner, wrapping it around filling.

9. Roll nori into a cone shape. Adhere seam of cone with 2 or 3 grains of sushi rice and press to seal. Serve with soy sauce.

Makes 12

salmon roe and cucumber hand rolls

6 sheets toasted nori, halved lengthwise
½ recipe sushi rice (pages 26–27)
wasabi
½ English (hothouse) cucumber, skin intact, seeds removed, cut into long, thin lengths
12 teaspoons salmon roe
Japanese soy sauce for serving

1. Place 1 half sheet of nori, shiny side down, in palm of one hand. Wet your other hand and place 2 heaping tablespoons sushi rice on left side of nori. Using wet fingertips, spread rice, flattening it with your fingers. Spread a little wasabi over rice.
2. Arrange 2 or 3 lengths of cucumber diagonally over rice from center to outer left corner. Spoon 1 teaspoon salmon roe near top left corner of roll.
3. Fold bottom left corner of nori toward top right corner, wrapping it around filling.
4. Roll nori into a cone shape. Adhere seam of cone with 2 or 3 grains of sushi rice and press to seal. Serve with soy sauce.

Makes 12

salmon and avocado hand rolls

6 sheets toasted nori, halved lengthwise
½ recipe sushi rice (pages 26–27)
wasabi
12 strips sashimi-quality salmon, each ½ inch
 (12 mm) thick x ½ inch (12 mm) wide x 3 inches
 (7.5 cm) long
1 small avocado, peeled, pitted and thinly sliced
Japanese soy sauce for serving

1. Place 1 half sheet of nori, shiny side down, in palm of one hand. Wet your other hand and place 2 heaping tablespoons sushi rice on left side of nori. Using wet fingertips, spread rice, flattening it with your fingers. Spread a little wasabi over rice.

2. Arrange 1 salmon strip and 2 or 3 avocado slices diagonally over rice from center to outer left corner.

3. Fold bottom left corner of nori toward top right corner, wrapping it around filling.

4. Roll nori into a cone shape. Adhere seam of cone with 2 or 3 grains of sushi rice and press to seal. Serve with soy sauce.

Makes 12

mini vegetarian hand rolls

Small hand rolls are easy to serve at parties and are equally easy for guests to eat with their hands. Other hand roll recipes can be modified to follow this method by cutting each nori sheet into quarters and dividing the filling ingredients accordingly.

3 scallions (shallots/spring onions)
1 carrot, peeled
¼ daikon, about 7 oz (220 g), peeled
5 sheets toasted nori, quartered
½ recipe sushi rice (pages 26–27)
10 teaspoons mayonnaise
**½ English (hothouse) cucumber, skin intact, seeds
 removed, cut into long, thin lengths**
2 teaspoons black sesame seeds
Japanese soy sauce for serving

1. Using a sharp knife, remove root end and dark top from each scallion. Cut into thin strips about 3 inches (7.5 cm) long. Place in a bowl of ice water until curled. Drain and set aside.

2. Finely shred carrot and daikon using a Japanese vegetable slicer. Place in separate bowls of ice water for 10 minutes. Drain.

3. Place 1 quarter sheet of nori, shiny side down, in palm of one hand. Wet your other hand and place 1 heaping tablespoon sushi rice on one half of nori. Using wet fingertips, spread rice, flattening it with your fingers. Spread ½ teaspoon mayonnaise over rice.

4. Arrange 2 cucumber strips diagonally over rice from center to outer left corner. Top with a little shredded carrot and daikon.

5. Fold bottom left corner of nori toward top right corner, wrapping it around filling.

6. Roll nori into a cone shape. Adhere seam of cone with 2 or 3 grains of sushi rice and press to seal. Decorate top of each roll with scallion curls and a sprinkle of sesame seeds. Serve with soy sauce

Makes 20

hand-formed sushi (nigiri-zushi)

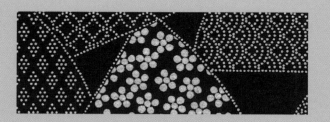

Hand-formed sushi, known as *nigiri-zushi*, is probably the hardest sushi to master. Although it looks simple to assemble, it is generally made by experienced sushi chefs.

Nigiri means "to squeeze." The word refers to the process of gently compressing a small amount of sushi rice into an oval shape, then adding a little wasabi and, finally, a topping, usually fresh fish. The perfect *nigiri-zushi* should be the right size to eat in one mouthful. The many traditional methods for preparing *nigiri-zushi* vary slightly from chef to chef.

Here is a quick method that home cooks can follow for making hand-formed sushi, along with some guidelines.

Allow 3 oz (90 g) fish per person.

Cut fish such as tuna and salmon on diagonal (page 28).

Prepare all ingredients before you start to assemble sushi.

Keep sushi rice covered with a damp towel to prevent it from drying out.

To facilitate handling sushi rice, combine 1 cup (8 fl oz/250 ml) water with 3 tablespoons rice vinegar in a bowl. Place the bowl near your work area and dip your hands in it before making each sushi.

salmon hand-formed sushi

½ recipe sushi rice (pages 26–27)
18 slices sashimi-quality salmon, each about ¼ inch
  (6 mm) thick x 1 inch (2.5 cm) wide x 2 inches
  (5 cm) long
wasabi

1. Dip your hands in vinegar water. Pick up a ball of sushi rice about size of a small chicken egg. Gently roll in palms of hands to form an oblong shape. Place on a clean board.
2. Spread each salmon slice with a little wasabi.
3. Hold rice shape in palm of one hand and place salmon slice, wasabi side down, on top. Cup sushi in palm and use 2 fingers of free hand to press gently on top of salmon to compact rice and salmon together. Then, using forefinger and thumb of free hand, squeeze sides together to shape and compact rice further. Repeat with remaining ingredients.

Makes 18
Note: Pictured page 100

1

2

3

4

103

omelet hand-formed sushi

½ recipe sushi rice (pages 26–27)
18 slices omelet (page 34), each ¼ inch
(6 mm) thick x 1 inch (2.5 cm) wide x 3 inches
(7.5 cm) long
18 nori bands (see below)
Japanese soy sauce for serving

1. Dip your hands in vinegar water. Pick up a ball of sushi rice about the size of a small chicken egg. Gently roll in palms of hands to form an oblong shape.
2. Cup rice shape in palm of one hand and use 2 fingers of free hand to press gently on top of rice to compact it. Then, using forefinger and thumb of free hand, squeeze sides together to shape and compact rice further. Place on a clean board and repeat with remaining rice.
3. Arrange 1 omelet slice on top of each sushi shape. Place a nori band around sushi. Repeat with remaining omelet slices and nori bands. Serve with soy sauce.

Makes 18

how to make nori bands

The topping can easily fall off hand-formed sushi. A band of nori holds the topping in place. Using kitchen scissors, cut a sheet of toasted nori into strips ½ inch (12 mm) wide x 3 inches (7.5 cm) long. Keep in a dry place until needed. Wrap 1 band around middle of each sushi so seam is on bottom. Use 2 grains of rice to seal seam.

tuna hand-formed sushi

Follow method for preparing salmon hand-formed sushi (page XX), substituting tuna slices for salmon. Serve with soy sauce.

Makes 18

½ recipe sushi rice (pages 26–27)
18 slices sashimi-quality tuna, each about ¼ inch
(6 mm) thick x 1 inch (2.5 cm) wide x
2 inches (5 cm) long
wasabi
Japanese soy sauce for serving

shrimp hand-formed sushi

18 jumbo shrimp (king prawns), cooked (page 30)
½ recipe sushi rice (pages 26–27)
wasabi
Japanese soy sauce for serving

Follow method for preparing salmon hand-formed sushi (page 102), substituting shrimp for salmon slices. Serve with soy sauce.

Makes 18

squid hand-formed sushi

Follow method for preparing salmon hand-formed sushi (page 102), substituting squid for salmon slices. Serve with soy sauce

Makes 18

½ recipe sushi rice (pages 26–27)
18 pieces squid body, each 1 inch (2.5 cm) wide x
3 inches (7.5 cm) long (page 18)
wasabi
Japanese soy sauce for serving

eel hand-formed sushi

½ recipe sushi rice (pages 26–27)
18 pieces cooked eel (page 18), each 1 inch (2.5 cm)
 wide x 3 inches (7.5 cm) long
18 nori bands (page 104)
Japanese soy sauce for serving

1. Dip your hands in vinegar water. Pick up a ball of sushi rice about size of a small chicken egg. Gently roll in palms of hands to form an oblong shape.
2. Hold rice shape in palm of one hand and place a piece of eel on top. Cup sushi in palm and use 2 fingers of free hand to press gently on top of eel to compact rice and eel together. Then, using forefinger and thumb of free hand, squeeze sides together to shape and compact rice further. Repeat with remaining ingredients. Place a nori band around each sushi. Serve with soy sauce.

Makes 18

asparagus hand-formed sushi

18 pencil-thin asparagus spears
½ recipe sushi rice (pages 26–27)
wasabi
18 nori bands (page 104)
Japanese soy sauce for serving

1. Bring a saucepan of water to a boil. Snap off tough ends from asparagus spears, then cut into 2-inch (5-cm) pieces. Plunge asparagus pieces in boiling water and cook for 1 minute. Drain asparagus and refresh in a bowl of ice water. Drain again and let cool completely.
2. Dip your hands in vinegar water. Pick up a ball of sushi rice about size of a small chicken egg. Gently roll in palms of hands to form an oblong shape.
3. Cup rice shape in palm of one hand and use 2 fingers of free hand to press gently on top of rice to compact it. Then, using forefinger and thumb of free hand, squeeze sides together to shape and compact rice further.
4. Place on a clean board and spread a little wasabi on top of rice. Arrange 3 asparagus pieces on top. Place a nori band around sushi. Repeat with remaining ingredients. Serve with soy sauce.

Makes 18
Note: Pictured opposite

shiitake mushroom hand-formed sushi

1. Remove white part from each scallion and discard or reserve for another use. Cut green tops of each scallion in half lengthwise to yield 2 strips. Trim each strip to 6 inches (15 cm) in length. Place scallion strips in a heatproof bowl, add boiling water to cover and let stand for 1 minute. Drain and set aside.

2. Place mushrooms in a heatproof bowl, add boiling water to cover and let stand for 20 minutes. Strain, reserving soaking liquid. Remove stems from mushrooms and discard. Place mushrooms, reserved liquid and dashi in a saucepan. Bring to a boil, reduce heat to low and simmer for 25 minutes. Remove from heat, stir in mirin and let cool to room temperature. Using a slotted spoon, remove mushrooms and set on paper towels to absorb excess moisture.

3. Dip your hands in vinegar water. Pick up a ball of sushi rice about size of a small chicken egg. Gently roll in palm of hands to form an oblong shape. Cup rice shape in palms of one hand and use 2 fingers of free hand to press gently on top of rice to compact it. Then, using forefinger and thumb of free hand, squeeze sides together to shape and compact rice further. Place on a clean board.

4. Place a mushroom on top of rice shape. Wrap a piece of scallion around mushroom and rice, tie in a knot and trim away excess scallion. Repeat with remaining ingredients. Serve with soy sauce.

Makes 18

9 scallions (shallots/spring onions)
18 dried shiitake mushrooms, each about 2 inches (5 cm) in diameter
1½ cups (12 fl oz/375 ml) dashi (page 142)
1 tablespoon mirin
½ recipe sushi rice (page 26–27)
Japanese soy sauce for serving

battleship sushi (gunkanmaki)

This sushi got its name because its profile resembles that of a battleship. Traditionally topped with fish roe, *gunkan-maki* can also be garnished with diced avocado or diced salmon or with a fresh oyster. The sushi should be prepared just before serving, as the nori quickly becomes soft.

3 sheets toasted nori
½ recipe sushi rice (pages 26–27)
wasabi
4 oz (125 g) red lumpfish caviar
3 oz (90 g) flying fish roe
6 oz (180 g) salmon roe
Japanese soy sauce for serving

1. Using a sharp knife or scissors, cut each nori sheet into 6 equal strips, each 1 inch (2.5 cm) wide and 6 inches (15 cm) long. You should have 18 strips.

2. Dip your hands in vinegar water. Pick up a ball of sushi rice about size of a small chicken egg. Gently roll in palms of hands to form an oblong shape slightly less than 1 inch (2.5 cm) thick. Place on a clean board and repeat with remaining rice.

3. Wrap a nori strip, shiny side out, around each rice shape. Use 1 or 2 grains of sushi rice to seal seam.

4. Dab a little wasabi across top of rice.

5. Spoon about 2 teaspoons caviar or roe onto rice. You will have 6 sushi made with caviar, 6 made with flying fish roe and 6 made with salmon roe. Serve with soy sauce.

Makes 18

crab battleship sushi

3 sheets toasted nori
1 lb (500 g) fresh crabmeat or drained canned
crabmeat
2 teaspoons lime juice
½ recipe sushi rice (page 26–27)
Wasabi
1 oz (30 g) salmon roe
Japanese soy sauce for serving

1. Using a sharp knife or scissors, cut each nori sheet into 6 equal strips, each 1 inch (2.5 cm) wide and 6 inches (15 cm) long. You should have 18 strips.
2. In a bowl, combine crabmeat and lime juice. Using a fork, mix well.
3. Dip your hands in vinegar water. Pick up a ball of sushi rice about size of a small chicken egg. Gently roll in palms of hands to form an oblong shape slightly less than 1 inch (2.5 cm) thick. Place on a clean board and repeat with remaining rice.
4. Wrap a nori strip, shiny side out, around each rice shape. Use 1 or 2 grains of sushi rice to seal seam.
5. Dab a little wasabi across top of rice.
6. Spoon about 1 tablespoon crab onto rice. Top with a little salmon roe. Repeat with remaining ingredients. Serve with soy sauce.

Makes 18

scattered sushi (chirashi-zushi)

tokyo sushi in a bowl

Scattered sushi is a good party or picnic dish, or family meal. It features a variety of sushi ingredients arranged on a platter or in a lacquerware bento, a Japanese lunch box which can be transported easily, and eaten with chopsticks.

8 jumbo shrimp (king prawns)

8 carrot flowers (page 38)

12 snowpeas (mange-tout), ends trimmed

½ recipe sushi rice (page 26–27)

4 slices canned or pickled lotus root, drained

4 shiso leaves

**6 oz (180 g) sashimi-quality tuna, cut into slices
   2 inches (12 mm) thick (page 28)**

**6 oz (180 g) sashimi-quality salmon fillet, cut into
   slices 2 inches (12 mm) thick (page 28)**

4 wasabi leaves (page 40)

4 cucumber pine branches (page 40)

4 fish roses, made with white-fleshed fish (page 38)

Japanese soy sauce for serving

1. Bring a saucepan of salted water to a boil. Add shrimp and cook until flesh turns white and bright pink, 2–3 minutes. Drain and refresh in a bowl of ice water. Drain again. Peel shrimp, leaving tails intact.

2. Using a sharp knife, cut along underside of each shrimp until you reach dark intestinal vein. Do not cut completely through shrimp. Remove vein with tip of knife. Briefly rinse shrimp under cold running water and pat dry with paper towels.

3. Using a knife or kitchen scissors, trim ends of shrimp tails, to neaten them.

4. Bring a small saucepan of water to a boil. Add carrot flowers and snowpeas and cook for 1 minute. Drain and refresh in a bowl of ice water. Drain again.

5. Divide sushi rice among 4 serving bowls. Arrange carrot flowers, snowpeas, lotus root and remaining ingredients attractively over rice, dividing them evenly among bowls. Serve with soy sauce.

Makes 4 servings

vegetarian scattered sushi (chirashi-zushi)

4 small dried shiitake mushrooms

2 carrots, peeled

2 scallions (shallots/spring onions)

4 snowpeas (mange-tout), ends trimmed and thinly sliced crosswise

8 asparagus spears, ends trimmed and cut into 2-inch (5-cm) pieces

8 green beans, ends trimmed and cut into 2 or 3 bite-sized pieces

2 deep-fried tofu skins

½ recipe sushi rice (page 26–27)

4 slices canned or pickled lotus root, drained

4 shiso leaves

1 teaspoon sesame seeds, toasted

Japanese soy sauce for serving

1. Place mushrooms in a heatproof bowl, add boiling water to cover and let stand for 20 minutes. Drain mushrooms, squeezing out any excess water. Remove stems from mushrooms and discard.

2. Finely shred carrots using a Japanese vegetable slicer. Place in a bowl of ice water and let stand for 10 minutes. Drain and pat dry with paper towels.

3. Using a sharp knife, remove root end and dark top from each scallion. Cut remaining section into thin strips about 3 inches (7.5 cm) long. Place in a bowl of ice water and let stand until curled, about 10 minutes. Drain.

4. Bring a saucepan of water to a boil. Add snowpeas, asparagus and green beans and cook for 1 minute. Drain and refresh in a bowl of ice water. Drain again.

5. Place tofu skins in a heatproof bowl, add boiling water to cover and let stand for 3 minutes to remove excess oil. Drain. Cut tofu skins into fine shreds.

6. Divide sushi rice among 4 serving bowls. Arrange mushrooms, carrots, scallions, snowpeas, asparagus, green beans, tofu skins, lotus root and shiso leaves attractivelyover rice, dividing them evenly among bowls. Sprinkle with sesame seeds. Serve with soy sauce.

Makes 4 servings

pressed sushi (oshi-zushi)

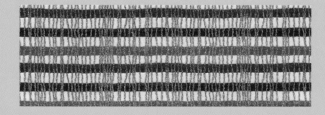

Pressed sushi, or *oshi-zushi*, is one of the oldest forms of sushi. It dates back to the 17th century before the advent of refrigeration, when fish and other ingredients were preserved by packing them into boxes with vinegared rice.

To make pressed sushi, you will need a sushi mold. The molds are available in wood or plastic and in many shapes and sizes. Wooden sushi molds should be soaked in cold water for at least 10 minutes, then wiped dry before using.

The recipe here uses a rectangular wooden mold measuring 6 inches (15 cm) long, 3 inches (7.5 cm) wide and 2 inches (5 cm) tall. If you do not have a sushi mold, you can use a springform pan about 8 inches (20 cm) in diameter and line it with plastic wrap to prevent the sushi rice from sticking. After removing the pan sides, you can trim the finished sushi to a square, then cut it into bite-sized squares or rectangles measuring about 1 x 2 inches (2.5 x 5 cm).

marinated mackerel pressed sushi

10 oz (300 g) mackerel fillets, marinated (page 32)
½ recipe sushi rice (pages 26–27)
Japanese soy sauce for serving
wasabi
pickled ginger for serving

1. Place mackerel fillets, skin side down, on a chopping board. Using a sharp knife, slice off thickest part of each fillet so fillet is nearly flat. Reserve any removed pieces of fish. Trim fillets to fit bottom of sushi mold, again reserving removed pieces.
2. Lay half of mackerel, skin side down, in a single layer in bottom of a sushi mold. Fill any gaps with reserved pieces.
3. Using wet hands, press half of sushi rice firmly on top of mackerel.
4. Place lid on mold and press down firmly to compact rice. Let stand for at least 10 minutes.

5. Holding lid down firmly, lift sides of mold up and over lid. Carefully remove lid. Invert bottom of mold holding rice and mackerel onto board. Carefully lift off bottom. Enclose mackerel and rice in plastic wrap and store in a cool place for up to 4 hours before serving. Rinse and dry mold thoroughly and repeat with remaining mackerel and sushi rice.
6. To serve, wet a sharp knife under cold running water. Cut each pressed sushi into 6 slices. Accompany with soy sauce, wasabi and pickled ginger.

Makes 12 slices

1

2

3

4

125

salmon pressed sushi

10 oz (300 g) sashimi-quality salmon
½ recipe sushi rice (see page 26–27)
wasabi
Japanese soy sauce for serving

1. Place salmon on a chopping board and cut into slices about 6 inches (15 cm) long, 3 inches (7.5 cm) wide and ⅛ inch (3 mm) thick (page 28). Reserve any small pieces. Lay half of salmon slices in a single layer in bottom of a sushi mold. Fill any gaps with reserved pieces.
2. Spread a little wasabi over salmon.
3. Using wet hands, press half of sushi rice firmly on top of salmon.
4. Place lid on mold and press down firmly to compact rice. Let stand for at least 10 minutes.
5. Holding lid down firmly, lift sides of mold up and over lid. Carefully remove lid. Invert bottom of mold holding rice and salmon onto board. Carefully lift off bottom. Enclose salmon and rice in plastic wrap and store in a cool place for up to 4 hours before serving. Rinse and dry mold thoroughly and repeat with remaining salmon, wasabi and sushi rice.
6. To serve, wet a sharp knife under cold running water. Cut each pressed sushi into 6 slices. Accompany with soy sauce.

Makes 12 slices

Variation: Substitute slices of smoked salmon or smoked rainbow trout for fresh salmon.

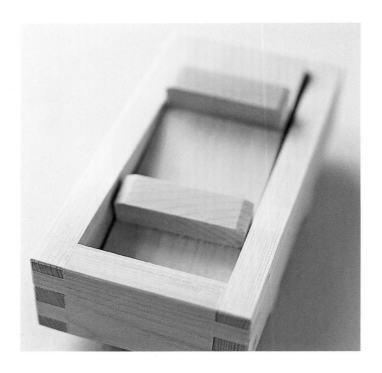

eel pressed sushi

10 oz (300 g) cooked eel, (page 18)
½ recipe sushi rice (pages 26–27)
Japanese soy sauce for serving

1. Place eel on a chopping board. Using a sharp knife, slice off thickest part of eel so it is nearly flat. Reserve any removed pieces of eel. Trim eel to fit bottom of sushi mold, reserving removed pieces.
2. Lay half of eel in a single layer in bottom of a sushi mold. Fill any gaps with reserved pieces.
3. Using wet hands, press half of sushi rice firmly on top of eel.
4. Place lid on mold and press down firmly to compact rice. Let stand for at least 10 minutes.
5. Holding lid down firmly, lift sides of mold up and over lid. Carefully remove lid. Invert bottom of mold holding rice and eel onto board. Carefully lift off bottom. Enclose eel and rice in plastic wrap and store in a cool place for up to 4 hours before serving. Rinse and dry mold thoroughly and repeat with remaining sushi rice and eel.
6. To serve, wet a sharp knife under cold running water. Cut each pressed sushi into 6 slices. Accompany with soy sauce.

Makes 12 slices

stuffed sushi (inari-zushi)

simple inari-zushi

For stuffed sushi, called *inari-zushi*, the Japanese use an array of cooked ingredients, such as omelets, deep-fried tofu skins and squid tubes, to hold the fillings. The fillings are generally a combination of sushi rice delicately flavored with soy sauce, mushrooms, scallions (shallots/spring onions) and/or sake. The tasty morsels are eaten as snacks or light meals, or are served as part of a sushi banquet.

5 deep-fried tofu skins
½ recipe dashi (page 142)
2 tablespoons sugar
2 teaspoons sake
2 tablespoons Japanese soy sauce
½ recipe sushi rice (pages 26–27)
½ teaspoon black sesame seeds (optional)
Japanese soy sauce for serving
pickled ginger for serving

1. Place tofu skins in a heatproof bowl, add boiling water to cover and let stand for 3 minutes to remove excess oil. Drain.
2. In a saucepan, combine dashi, sugar, sake and soy sauce. Bring to a boil, reduce heat to low, add tofu skins and simmer, uncovered, for 10 minutes. Using a slotted spoon, remove tofu skins and drain. Discard dashi.
3. Place tofu skins on a chopping board. Cut each in half.
4. Carefully open each half to create a pocket. If you cannot open pocket, place tofu on board and roll gently with a rolling pin. Wet your hands and pick up a ball of rice slightly smaller than a golf-ball. Gently squeeze rice into an oblong and carefully insert in a tofu pocket. Do not overfill pocket or it will split.
5. Wrap edges of pocket opening over rice and place filled pocket seam side down. Repeat with remaining pockets and sushi rice. Sprinkle with sesame seeds, if desired. Serve with soy sauce and pickled ginger.

Makes 10

1

2

3

4

133

stuffed squid sushi

3 squid, each about 5 oz (150 g)

3 tablespoons rice vinegar

2 tablespoons Japanese soy sauce

3 dried shiitake mushrooms

½ recipe sushi rice (pages 26–27)

2 teaspoons peeled and grated fresh ginger

3 scallions (shallots/spring onions), white parts only, finely chopped

3 shiso leaves, finely chopped

Japanese soy sauce for serving

1. Clean and prepare squid as directed on page 18, keeping squid bodies whole and reserving tentacles. Place bodies and tentacles in a large saucepan with water to cover. Add vinegar and soy sauce. Bring to a boil over medium heat, reduce heat to low and simmer until squid turns white, about 2 minutes. Be careful not to overcook squid or it will become tough. Drain and let cool. Chop tentacles and set aside.

2. Place mushrooms in a heatproof bowl, add boiling water to cover and let stand for 20 minutes. Drain. Remove stems from mushrooms and discard. Chop mushroom caps.

3. In a large bowl, combine tentacles, mushrooms, sushi rice, ginger, scallions and shiso. Using a fork, mix until well combined.

4. Tightly fill each squid body with rice mixture. Enclose each stuffed squid in plastic wrap and let stand at room temperature for 30 minutes. Cut into slices about ¼ inch (6 mm) wide. Serve with soy sauce.

Makes 3

omelet stuffed sushi

For each sushi, a thin omelet is folded around sushi rice and resembles a Japanese napkin used at a traditional tea ceremony.

4 scallions (shallots/spring onions)
4 dried shiitake mushrooms
2 tablespoons sugar
1 tablespoon mirin
1 tablespoon sake
1 tablespoon Japanese soy sauce
1 carrot, peeled and finely chopped
½ recipe sushi rice (pages 26–27)
3 teaspoons sesame seeds, toasted
10 eggs
pinch salt
2 tablespoons canola oil
Japanese soy sauce for serving

1. Remove white part from each scallion and discard or reserve for another use. Cut green tops of each scallion in half lengthwise to yield 2 strips. Trim each strip to 6 inches (15 cm) in length. Place scallion strips in a heatproof bowl, add boiling water to cover and let stand for 1 minute. Drain and set aside.

2. Place mushrooms in a heatproof bowl, add boiling water to cover and let stand for 20 minutes. Strain, reserving soaking liquid. Remove stems from mushrooms and discard. Chop mushroom caps.

3. In a small saucepan, combine ⅓ cup (3 fl oz/90 ml) reserved soaking liquid, 1 tablespoon sugar, mirin, sake and soy sauce. Bring to a boil, add chopped mushrooms and carrot, reduce heat to low and simmer until nearly all liquid is absorbed, about 3 minutes. Let cool.

4. In a bowl, combine sushi rice, mushroom mixture and sesame seeds. Using a fork, mix until well combined.

5. In a large bowl, lightly beat eggs with a fork. Strain through a sieve into another bowl. Add 1 tablespoon sugar and salt. Stir to combine.

6. In an 8-inch (20-cm) square frying pan (page 34) over medium heat, warm oil. Using chopsticks and paper towel, wipe excess oil from pan. Set paper towel aside.

7. Pour one-eighth of egg mixture in pan to cover bottom. Cook until surface begins to set. Using a spatula, turn omelet and cook until until firm, but not brown. Transfer to a plate and let cool. Repeat with remaining egg mixture, using oil-soaked paper towel to coat surface of pan.

8. Place an omelet on a chopping board so one point of square is toward you. Wet your hands and pick up a ball of rice slightly larger than than a golf-ball. Place rice in center of omelet and gently flatten. Fold corner of omelet closest to you over rice, then fold corner farthest from you over rice. Finally, fold right and left corners over rice, to resemble back of an envelope.

9. Turn omelet seam side down. Wrap a strip of scallion around omelet, tie in a knot and trim excess. Repeat with remaining ingredients. Serve with soy sauce.

Makes 8

soups

clear soup with shrimp

A small bowl of clear soup, or *suimono*, is traditionally served at the beginning, middle or end of a Japanese meal to help cleanse the palate. Just before serving, the ingredients are placed in a small bowl and hot dashi is poured over them. The ingredients are chosen for their flavor and for their artistic presentation, which should be pleasing to the eye.

4 jumbo shrimp (king prawns), peeled and deveined, heads intact (optional) and tails intact

1 small carrot, peeled

1 scallion (shallot/spring onion)

1 recipe dashi (page 142)

salt to taste

sake to taste

Japanese soy sauce for serving

1. Bring a small saucepan of water to a boil. Add shrimp and cook until flesh turns bright pink and white, about 2 minutes. Drain.

2. Finely shred carrot using a Japanese vegetable slicer. Place in a bowl of ice water and let stand for 10 minutes. Drain.

3. Using a sharp knife, remove root end and dark top from scallion. Cut remaining section into thin strips about 3 inches (7.5 cm) long. Place in a bowl of ice water and let stand until curled, about 10 minutes. Drain.

4. Place dashi in a saucepan and bring to a boil over medium heat. Season with salt and sake.

5. Divide shredded carrot among 4 serving bowls. Place a shrimp in each bowl. Pour hot dashi over shrimp and carrot, dividing evenly. Garnish each serving with scallion curls. Accompany with soy sauce.

Serves 4

miso soup with tofu

2 tablespoons white miso paste

1 tablespoon hot water

1 recipe dashi (below)

4 oz (125 g) firm tofu, drained and cut into ½-inch (12-mm) cubes

4 snowpeas (mange-tout), ends trimmed and thinly sliced

Japanese soy sauce for serving

1. In a small cup, mix together miso and hot water until blended.
2. Place dashi in a saucepan and add miso. Bring to a boil over medium heat, reduce heat to low and simmer for 3 minutes.
3. Divide tofu and snowpeas among 4 serving bowls. Pour hot dashi over tofu and snowpeas, dividing evenly. Accompany with soy sauce.

Serves 4

dashi

1 piece kombu, about 4 inches (10 cm) long

4 cups (32 fl oz/1 L) water

2 cups (½ oz/15 g) dried bonito flakes, loosely packed

1. Wipe kombu with a damp kitchen towel to remove any white film on surface. Using scissors, make a few cuts into kombu to help release its flavor as it cooks.
2. In a large saucepan, combine water and kombu. Bring to a boil over medium heat. Remove kombu and discard.
3. Add bonito flakes to saucepan but do not stir. Bring to a boil over medium heat, then remove from heat.
4. Let dashi stand for 3 minutes. Pour through a strainer lined with cheesecloth (muslin) and set over another saucepan. Discard cheesecloth and bonito. If you prefer stronger-flavored dashi, simmer, uncovered, over medium heat for 10 minutes.

clear soup with white fish

2 scallions (shallots/spring onions)
1 recipe dashi (page 142)
1 tablespoon Japanese soy sauce
1 tablespoon mirin
8 oz (250 g) white-fleshed fish fillets, such as sea
   bass, snapper or bream, skin intact, cut into
   8 pieces
4 snowpeas (mange-tout), ends trimmed and thinly
   sliced crosswise
Japanese soy sauce for serving

1. Using a sharp knife, remove root end and dark top from each
   scallion. Cut remaining section into thin strips about 3 inches
   (7.5 cm) long. Place in a bowl of ice water until curled, about
   10 minutes. Drain.
2. Place dashi in a saucepan and bring to a boil over medium heat.
   Add soy sauce, mirin and fish, remove from heat and let stand for
   5 minutes.
3. Divide fish and snowpeas among 4 serving bowls. Pour hot dashi
   over fish and snowpeas, dividing evenly. Garnish each serving with
   scallion curls. Accompany with soy sauce.

Serves 4

sushi etiquette

The eating of sushi and sashimi follows traditional practices. The Japanese generally start a meal with small bowls of hot clear soup. Afterward, a beautiful arrangement of sashimi, accompanied by pickled ginger, wasabi and soy sauce, is brought to the table, followed by a selection of sushi. According to tradition, small bowls of hot clear soup are also served during and at the end of a meal to cleanse the palate.

Wasabi, an essential accompaniment to sashimi or sushi, should be used sparingly, so it enhances the food, instead of overpowering it. Similarly, food should be dipped lightly in soy sauce rather than soaked in it, which can cause the sushi to disintegrate and leave rice in the dipping bowl. When eating hand-formed sushi, it is considered impolite to dip it in the soy sauce, take one bite, then return it to your plate. The entire piece of sushi should be eaten in one mouthful. Pickled ginger is consumed a slice at a time to cleanse the palette between eating different flavors.

When setting the table for a sushi meal, provide a plate, a small dipping bowl for soy sauce and a set of chopsticks for each guest. Each place setting should also include a chopstick rest, which lifts the tips of the chopsticks above the table. These small rests are made in various shapes—whether a small rectangle or a recognizable form like a fish—generally from wood, porcelain or bamboo. The two chopsticks should be aligned side by side in front of the plate, with their ends on the rest, facing left. The Japanese believe it is bad luck to orient the chopstick tips to the right. Finally, place a Japanese teacup next to each setting, as it is customary to serve each guest a cup of hot green tea on arriving.

As when making sushi, it is important to create a table setting with harmony and balance through the use of color and texture. Small bowls of pickled ginger can be neatly arranged on the table for guests to share. Soy sauce can be served in small attractive bottles or bowls, and neat mounds of wasabi can be set on individual plates. For a particularly artistic presentation, the wasabi can be formed into leaf shapes (page 40).

Japanese chopsticks have very pointed ends, to help diners adroitly pick up delicate pieces of fish and rice, unlike Chinese chopsticks, which have blunt ends. Keep in mind that passing food from your chopsticks to another person's chopsticks is believed to invite bad luck. When selecting food from a serving platter of sushi, it is considered polite to use the wide ends rather than the pointed ends. Chopsticks should be placed on their rest between courses, not on the plate or directly on the table.

beverages to serve with sushi

The most traditional beverage is a small cup of hot Japanese green tea *(agari)*. It cleanses the palate and acts as a gentle aid to digestion. In Japan, a cup of green tea is always offered when guests sit down to the table. Their cups are kept filled throughout the meal.

Sake, another traditional beverage, has a smooth taste that enhances the clean flavors of Japanese food. It is generally served at room temperature or slightly chilled. Some like to serve it hot. Sake has a high alcoholic content; when heated, it becomes even more potent. The price of sake usually indicates the quality. For special occasions, sake can be decanted into a beautiful ceramic or wooden serving bottle and poured into individual tiny matching cups.

A glass of cold beer is also a refreshing accompaniment to sushi and sashimi. Beer brewed in Japan is increasingly available in other countries. Chilled white wines such as Sauvignon Blanc and Chardonnay, as well as sparkling white wines, also complement sushi. Guests who are imbibing sake, beer or wine should also be served green tea.

sushi trouble shooting

rice sticks to fingers

In a bowl, combine 1 cup (8 fl oz/250 ml) water with 3 tablespoons rice vinegar. Place bowl near your work area and dip your hands in vinegar water to moisten them and prevent rice from sticking.

nori used for rolled sushi has split

This common problem has four possible causes—too much rice was spread on nori; rice was spread too close to far edge, causing seam to open; too much filling was placed in roll; filling was too moist. To save a split sushi roll, place a nori sheet of same size on a bamboo mat, then set split roll at one end of new sheet, pick up edge of mat and roll.

filling in rolled sushi is loose

Make sure you hold filling firmly with fingertips as you roll bamboo mat.

filling in rolled sushi is off center

Filling was positioned incorrectly. Remember to arrange filling ingredients in center of rice.

pressed sushi is stuck in mold

Wooden sushi molds need to be soaked in cold water for 10 minutes before use. A wet knife can be slipped between sushi and sides of mold before lifting sides. If using another mold such as a plastic food-storage container to make molded sushi, line it with plastic wrap.

glossary

While I may not have used all of the following items, these are the ingredients you will come across in Japanese stores while shopping for sushi ingredients. Once you have mastered the techniques in this book, expand your repertoire and experiment with other ingredients and recipes.

Aka oroshi: Japanese red chili paste. This is mixed with grated daikon radish and used as a garnish for white-fish sushi.

Ao-nori: Edible green seaweed. Sold in dried flake form. It is usually sprinkled when served, so it is not too moist when eaten.

Asian sesame oil: A fragrant, richly colored oil made from sesame seeds. Only small quantities of Asian sesame oil are required for flavoring.

Bamboo leaves: Inedible garnish, often used when fish is placed on top of leaf. Bamboo leaves need sustained moisture and should be kept in water until needed.

Bamboo shoots: Tender but crispy shoots, available in cans from most stores. Used for texture rather than flavor.

Beni-shoga: Pickled red ginger made with older season ginger. More savory than the pink variety (gari). Available sliced or shredded in packets or jars.

Blanched cabbage leaves: Rinse leaves to remove dirt and microwave 1–2 minutes, or simmer in boiling water until leaves just soft, 1–2 minutes. Immediately rinse under cold water to stop the cooking process.

Blanched spinach leaves: Rinse leaves to remove dirt and microwave 1–2 minutes, or simmer in boiling water until leaves just soft, 1–2 minutes. Immediately rinse under cold water to stop the cooking process and set color.

Cellophane noodles: Also known as bean thread or harusame noodles. Gossamer, translucent threads are made from the starch of green mung beans, potato starch or sweet potato starch. They are sold dried and so must be soaked in hot water to soften before using.

Chili mayonnaise: This is chili added to Japanese mayonnaise. Use either chili paste or fresh chilies, and add as much or as little as desired. Chili mayonnaise is particularly suitable for chicken.

Chili oil: Vegetable oil infused with chilies to obtain their flavor and heat. Often tinged red, there are many varieties of chili oil available in both Asian markets and supermarkets. It will keep for up to 6 months at room temperature, but retains its flavor better if stored in the refrigerator.

Chili peppers: As a general rule, the smaller the chili the hotter the flavor regardless of the color. Remove seeds and membranes to reduce heat.

Chili sauce or sweet chili sauce: Although not traditional, this spicy blend of tomatoes, chilies and onions can be used as a dipping sauce in or with sushi.

Cilantro: Also known as coriander or Chinese parsley. Available fresh, the roots, stems and leaves are all used in cooking. The leaves are used for garnishing and are strongly flavored, so use sparingly.

Dashi: This traditional Japanese stock, which is made from bonito fish flakes (katsuobushi) and kombu (seaweed), is the basis of many Japanese dishes. Granules or liquid instant dashi is readily available. If a completely vegetarian stock is required, use only kombu and double the quantity.

Dried somen noodles: Thin, white noodles made from wheat flour.

Egg mimosa: Sieved egg yolk cooked until hard (hard-boiled), used for sprinkling or a decoration such as the stamen in a carved radish flower. To make 1 teaspoon of egg mimosa, place a fresh egg in a pot of water.

Bring water to a boil and simmer for 15 minutes until egg is hard-boiled. Remove egg shell under running water and when egg is chilled, remove egg white. Place egg yolk in a sieve. Pressing with a teaspoon, sieve into a small bowl.

Enoki mushrooms: Also called enokitake mushrooms, these are pale colored with long thin stalks topped by tiny caps. They have a mild flavor and crunchy texture. Fresh mushrooms may be purchased in Asian markets and some supermarkets. Trim the root ends of the stalks before using.

Fish sauce: Pungent sauce of salted, fermented fish and other seasonings, used in cooking and as a dipping sauce. Products vary in intensity based on the country of origin.

Fu: Wheat gluten in small decorative shapes. Sold dried.

Gari: Pickled pink ginger made with early season ginger. Sweeter than the red variety (beni-shoga). Available sliced in packets and jars. Served with sushi for cleansing the palate in between dishes.

Green curry paste: This is suitable for sushi made with fresh vegetables or fruit.

Green-ginger juice: Peel a green ginger and grate into a bowl. Squeeze with fingers to make green-ginger juice.

Ichimi togarashi: Ground chili powder used as a seasoning (see also shichimi togarashi).

Japanese mayonnaise: Japanese mayonnaise is creamy and less sweet than western mayonnaise. For more bite, add wasabi to make wasabi mayonnaise.

Kanten (agar): Also called agar-agar, this is a tasteless dried seaweed used as a setting agent, much like gelatine. It is available in blocks, powders or strands.

Kelp: Large dark brown seaweed sold dry. When using, rinse kelp and soak in water. Kelp is highly nutritious, but it is seldom eaten on its own.

Kinome: Japanese pepper; the sprigs provide an aromatic additional flavor. They are an edible garnish or herbal ingredient.

Konnyaku: Devil's tongue jelly. Made from konnyaku potato and formed either into bricks or strings.

Matcha: Green tea. A green powdered tea with a bitter yet pleasant taste. This tea is indispensable in a Japanese tea ceremony.

Mitsuba: Used as a herb in soups and salads, mitsuba, also known as Japanese wild chervil, is a form of parsley, which can be substituted. The tastes, however, are not identical; the flavor of mitsuba is somewhat like that of celery.

Myoga: Japanese ginger, but has quite a different herbal fragrance than ginger when sliced thinly as a sashimi condiment.

Sansho: Japanese pepper, bitter tasting.

Shichimi togarashi: Seven spice mix, based on hot peppers. Used as a seasoning.

Shimeji mushrooms: Clusters of straw-colored mushrooms with small heads. Use in soups and nabemono (one-pot dishes).

Shiromiso: White miso, with a pale yellow color, a sweet flavor, and a salt content that varies from 5 to 10 percent.

Soba noodles: Noodles made from buckwheat flour, wheat flour and sometimes powdered green tea.

Tempura flour (tenpura ko): This flour comes in many variations, but is basically a mixture of eggs, wheat flour and iced water. The ingredients are combined only lightly until a lumpy batter full of air bubbles forms. If the batter settles during food preparation, it should be replaced with a new batch.

Tobiko: Preserved flying fish roe. A very thin texture, and a sparkling orange color.

Ugo: Salted green seaweed, sold in a packet. Rinse well, before using.

Wakame: A type of seaweed available in dried form that is reconstituted in water and becomes bright green. Wakame is used in soups, salads, simmered dishes, and is finely chopped and mixed through rice. Dried wakame must be soaked before using.

index

guide to weights and measures

The metric weights and metric fluid measures used in this book are those of Standards Australia. All cup and spoon measurements are level:

- The Australian Standard measuring cup has a capacity of 250 millilitres (250 ml).
- The Australian Standard tablespoon has a capacity of 20 millilitres (20 ml).

In all recipes metric equivalents of imperial measures are shown in parentheses e.g. 1 lb (500 g) beef. For successful cooking use either metric or imperial weights and measures—do not mix the two.

weights

Imperial	Metric
$^1/_3$ oz	10 g
$^1/_2$ oz	15 g
$^3/_4$ oz	20 g
1 oz	30 g
2 oz	60 g
3 oz	90 g
4 oz ($^1/_4$ lb)	125 g
5 oz ($^1/_3$ lb)	150 g
6 oz	180 g
7 oz	220 g
8 oz ($^1/_2$ lb)	250 g
9 oz	280 g
10 oz	300 g
11 oz	330 g
12 oz ($^3/_4$ lb)	375 g
16 oz (1 lb)	500 g
2 lb	1 kg
3 lb	1.5 kg
4 lb	2 kg

volume

Imperial	Metric	Cup
1 fl oz	30 ml	
2 fl oz	60 ml	$^1/_4$
3 fl oz	90 ml	$^1/_3$
4 fl oz	125 ml	$^1/_2$
5 fl oz	150 ml	$^2/_3$
6 fl oz	180 ml	$^3/_4$
8 fl oz	250 ml	1
10 fl oz	300 ml	$1^1/_4$
12 fl oz	375 ml	$1^1/_2$
13 fl oz	400 ml	$1^2/_3$
14 fl oz	440 ml	$1^3/_4$
16 fl oz	500 ml	2
24 fl oz	750 ml	3
32 fl oz	1 L	4

oven temperature guide

The Celsius (°C) and Fahrenheit (°F) temperatures in this chart apply to most electric ovens. Decrease by 25°F or 10°C for a gas oven or refer to the manufacturer's temperature guide. For temperatures below 325°F (160°C), do not decrease the given temperature.

Oven description	°C	°F	Gas Mark
Cool	110	225	$^1/_4$
	130	250	$^1/_2$
Very slow	140	275	1
	150	300	2
Slow	170	325	3
Moderate	180	350	4
	190	375	5
Moderately Hot	200	400	6
Fairly Hot	220	425	7
Hot	230	450	8
Very Hot	240	475	9
Extremely Hot	250	500	10

useful conversions

$^1/_4$ teaspoon	1.25 ml
$^1/_2$ teaspoon	2.5 ml
1 teaspoon	5 ml
1 Australian tablespoon	20 ml (4 teaspoons)
1 UK/US tablespoon	15 ml (3 teaspoons)

Butter/Shortening		
1 tablespoon	$^1/_2$ oz	15 g
$1^1/_2$ tablespoons	$^3/_4$ oz	20 g
2 tablespoons	1 oz	30 g
3 tablespoons	$1^1/_2$ oz	45 g